READING THE YOUNG MARX AND ENGELS

Reading the Young Marx and Engels

POETRY, PARODY AND THE CENSOR

MARGARET A. ROSE

CROOM HELM LONDON

ROWMAN AND LITTLEFIELD TOTOWA N.J.

© 1978 Margaret Rose
Croom Helm Ltd, 2-10 St John's Road, London SW11

British Library Cataloguing in Publication Data

Rose, Margaret
    Reading the young Marx and Engels.
    1. Marx, Karl
    I. Title
    838'.7'09   PT2428.M47Z/

    ISBN 0−85664−792−6

First published in the United States 1978 by
Rowman and Littlefield
81 Adams Drive, Totowa, New Jersey

ISBN 0−8476−6087−7

Printed in Great Britain by
Biddles Ltd, Guildford, Surrey

CONTENTS

ACKNOWLEDGEMENTS

I take this opportunity to thank the History of Ideas Unit of the Australian National University, Canberra, and the University itself, for the Research Fellowship which enabled me to work on the following study during 1977, and the Alexander von Humboldt Stiftung for the opportunity to work in libraries and institutes in Germany and in Amsterdam in 1978.

My thanks also go to Dr F.B. Smith for reading the manuscript, to those who listened and advised and, in particular, to Professor Sidney Monas for his discussion of the problem of censorship.

To May McKenzie, Vibeke Wetselaar, Jan Grocott and Minh-Thu Ajkic, who helped type the manuscript with such special speed and accuracy, go my most grateful acknowledgement and thanks.

Auf, auf, ihr Freien all! Was sitzt ihn an den Kunkeln,
Wenn die Romantiker die Welt ringsum verdunkeln?
Wenn die Reaktion sich reget, wenn verschmitzt
Der Wissenschaft schon halb sie im Nacken sitzt?
Der Bauer ist bedroht; an wütige Zensoren
Geht, was ihr denkt und schreibt, zum grössten Teil verloren;
Drum Freie allesamt, horcht meinem Manifest,
Vorausgesetzt dass es der Zensor drucken lässt:
Es ist jetzt hohe Zeit, dass wir als Diplomaten
Die heil'ge Allianz ernst im Kongress beraten.
Seht ihr, wie sie sich müht, die hohe Polizei,
Zu tilgen überall das kleine Wörtchen frei?

Friedrich Engels, *Der Triumph des Glaubens*,
1842, MEGA, I/2, p. 267.

PREFACE

The republication of Marx's poetic works and other juvenilia by the Moscow Institute for Marxism-Leninism in 1975[1] has reopened one of the more obscure areas of Marx scholarship. The very reasons for the obscurity of this early period in Marx's writing life are in themselves interesting, and will be related in this study to the two forms of censorship which have contributed to the silencing of Marx's poetry in his lifetime and since, to the censorship of the liberal poets of the Young Germany in 1835 when the 17-year-old Marx began writing the verse we now have, and to his own rejection of his poetic works in 1837 as 'Romantic moonshine', a rejection which has continued to influence the negative reception of the juvenilia by Marx scholars.

The poetic inadequacies of Marx's verses have also led literary critics to avoid spending much if any time with them. Most use has been made of them by such serious biographers as Auguste Cornu and, more recently, David McClellan, but they have also been used by psycho-biographers such as Robert Payne and Arnold Künzli to argue for the existence of pathological traits in the young Marx. Here misunderstandings of Marx's use of various personae, as well as of his imitation of other authors, have combined with a lack of awareness of the effect on Marx's generation of the ban put on the Young German poets in 1835, and have produced a picture of the young Marx which a more careful analysis of both the literary text and its social context must clarify and correct.

Recent work by Heinz Monz,[2] has produced much new and interesting information about Marx's schooling in Trier under the Kantian Wyttenbach. Nicolaevsky and Maenchen-Helfen had pointed out in their earlier biography[3] that Wyttenbach's career as a Jacobin sympathiser had extended into the 1830s (when Marx was a student in Trier) to supporting a poetic circle named after the Young Germany, as well as to being involved with other movements sympathetic to the July Revolution, before he was dismissed from his directorship in November 1835. Monz's researches in Trier confirm and amplify such findings.

The following study seeks to place the poetry into the context of the censorship of Marx's contemporaries in the 1830s, into the history of censorship in Prussia since the Enlightenment, about which Marx

11

writes his first published article early in 1842 and into the context of Trier, in which Marx was a student until the end of 1835. Parody — one of the most popular nineteenth-century methods of 'smuggling' ideas past the censor — is studied as a central stylistic device in the work of both Marx and Engels. Both had continued to use it, in different ways, into the 1840s, in works such as *The Holy Family* and *The German Ideology*. The problematical role of parody in these works, and in the hypothesised 'epistemological break' of 1845, before its replacement by more exact and 'scientific' methods, is one of the central issues of Part Two of the study. In the study as a whole both the conditions of and form taken by the 'silences' in Marx's early texts — the absence of issues banned by the censor or their circumlocution in parody — are related to the historical background of the juvenilia, to Marx's subsequent development, and to the reception of his poetic works in the present century. In this way an 'esoteric' reading of Marx's juvenilia is suggested which takes into account both text and context. Bridging the disciplines of literary history and theory, philosophy, and the social sciences, the subject dealt with in this study — of the effects of censorship on Marx's early works — requires new consideration tolerant of its interdisciplinary character.

Notes

1. See Bibliography for details of this new edition of the MEGA, the Marx/ Engels Gesamtausgabe (herein referred to as the 'New MEGA'). Some of the poems (of 1836/7) appeared in English in the Lawrence and Wishart edition in 1975.

2. Heinz Monz, *Karl Marx — Grundlagen der Entwicklung zu Leben und Werk*, 2nd edn. of *Karl Marx und Trier*, Trier, 1973.

3. Boris Nicolaevsky and Otto Maenchen-Helfen, *Karl Marx: Man and Fighter* (1935), Harmondsworth, 1976.

Part One

CENSORSHIP AND MARX'S POETIC WRITINGS

1.1 CENSORSHIP AND THE ENLIGHTENMENT TRADITION

Marx's first published article was on the new instruction on the freedom of the press authorised by Friedrich Wilhelm IV of Prussia on 24 December 1841. In that essay Marx takes up issues raised in the 1780s by Enlightenment decrees on censorship, which (like those made by Friedrich Wilhelm IV in 1840 and 1841) purported to loosen the state's control over its writers. The relevance of Marx's discussion of censorship to his poetry is twofold. For not only was his poetry written against a background of debates on censorship in the 1830s, when Friedrich Wilhelm III was enforcing stricter control in the wake of the July Revolutions, but it was also composed under the threat of censorship of any writings sympathetic to or based on the Young German authors banned in 1835. Marx's use of older eighteenth-century Romantic authors as his models in his poetic works must be viewed against this background.

Though the Prussian King Friedrich Wilhelm IV began his reign with gestures imitative of Frederick the Great's Enlightenment, such as the new press instruction of December 1841, these were not maintained for very long, and important differences between the eighteenth-century Enlightenment experience with censorship and the nineteenth-century situation soon became obvious. As Ulla Otto[1] writes, Frederick the Great (Friedrich II) had, early in his reign, on his own initiative and against the advice of others, allowed a newspaper to appear uncensored. Though, as Otto points out, this was also accompanied by new censorship restrictions, it came to represent the Enlightenment 'thaw' of government control over literature in the period of Absolutism, which was also embodied in the reforms of the Habsburg Emperor Joseph II.[2]

The Enlightenment belief in Reason, and in the power of literature to represent the aims of the rational state, is also represented in the brief thaw of censorship restrictions instituted in the 1780s by Joseph II. In order to identify itself with the intellectuals, writers, and literati representing Reason, the state had not only to control their work but to show understanding of its integrity, if not its autonomy. The Enlightenment censor, drawn from the ranks of writers and intellectuals whose work he was to oversee, represented the 'internalisation' of the object of censorship within the process of censorship itself. This was but one aspect of the attempt by the state both to control and to empathise with the intellectual world. It might also be seen as reflecting the eighteenth-century belief in 'private censure' and a moral code based on the principle of self-rule, but which was itself enforced by public pressure.

In the late eighteenth century, the state had also used institutions such as the censor to confer its identity on its citizens, so that their 'autonomy' was actually both state-given and of the state in character. Writing from within the Habsburg Empire at the end of the nineteenth century Freud reflected the pervasiveness of these attitudes in using the term 'censor' to describe the mechanisms of repression at work in the psyche, and in giving the super-ego a significant role to play in the development of the individual's sense of identity. And yet the enlightened state also came to see that this emphasis on individuality must lead to a conflict between itself and the individuals seeking self-expression within it. The demand for the right to freedom of speech made in 1789 represents a new form of the individual's drive for independence, and was to create difficulties for the 'thaw' instituted in Prussia and Vienna in the 1780s. It was in 1789 that Friedrich Wilhelm II, for example, attempted to introduce a censorship instruction to revoke Frederick's reforms.

In his *Zensuredikt* of 11 June 1781, Joseph II had decreed that the state was open to criticism from its subjects. Otto writes, 'Der gesamte Staat wird in seinen Vertretern justiziabel vor dem Urteil der Öffentlichkeit'.[3] This dialogue of the state with its citizens had, however, the function of giving the state the role of interlocutor with its people: 'Der Hof partizipiert in der Weise an der öffentlichen Kommunikation, dass er die *vox populi* als Korrektur anzuhören bereit ist.' By means of such concepts as the *Volkszensur*[4] — censorship in which the public conscience, the voice of the people, might play a role — the state could both maintain control over censorship, and thus over its writers, and appear in a non-tyrannical role, while also making the *vox populi* in part responsible for the judgements of the censor. (One form of 'Volkszensur' suggested was censorship ratified by a jury of citizens.) Just as the writer was internalised into the state as censor, so the state attempted, by encouraging criticism from its citizens, to be internalised in them, but as a controlling power.

The French Revolution, with its claims for the right to free speech, broke with the Enlightenment belief in the necessity for state control over writing, and with the idea of conferring the identity of the state upon its citizens. The new individualism of the revolutionary period represented both the extension of the Enlightenment belief in Liberty and Reason, and rejection of the subjugation of the individual to the identity of the monarchic state and to *its* understanding of Freedom and Reason. The individualism of the nineteenth century is reflected in Marx's argument against censorship in 1842 that the censor both steals the individual identity of the writer and creates hypocrisy in literature in 'writing over' another's style. In his articles against censorship, written in 1842, Marx also contradicted views such as those put forward by the eighteenth-century censor Sonnenfels,[5] that censorship improved a writer's style by forcing him to take greater care with what he wrote. But, more than this, Marx's defence of the individuality of the writer repeats the French Revolution's reaction to the eighteenth-century sanctification of the role of the censor, which was, with other nineteenth-century developments, to spell the end of Friedrich Wilhelm's attempt to play the role of Frederick the Great. The revolutions of the nineteenth century had also shown the monarchs of Europe that the making of laws could be threatened from below, and that those controlling the organs of public opinion, such as the popular press, showed no desire to assume the identity of the state at the expense of their own. Thus Friedrich Wilhelm IV found that his repetition of Frederick the Great's 'thaw' of censorship regulations was met in the 1840s with a liberation of dissent with which he could not cope.

Friedrich Wilhelm IV's professed respect for the writers and intellectuals of Prussia was, like his criticism of too restrictive a censorship, soon silenced. Cut off from the liberal intellectuals and writers of his time by this silence, Friedrich Wilhelm IV's reaction was to quieten their criticism by new and stricter censorship restrictions. The individualism of writers, which the state had once attempted to mould by a 'liberalisation' of censorship, was, in 1843, made the subject of new attacks. Journals such as the *Rheinische Zeitung*, previously allowed, were now censored severely and even banned entirely.

As Reisner writes in his useful study of censorship in Germany in the 1840s,[6] the control of censorship in Prussia had been so divided before February 1843, that journals and publications on or concerning contemporary political issues were the province of the Ministry for the Exterior, theological and scientific works that of the Ministry for Religion and Public Education, while all other matters were under the control of the Police Department of the Ministry for Internal Affairs. After February 1843 these areas of control were centralised under the

Ministry for Internal Affairs (the *Innenministerium*) the minister of
which became head of the school of censors. Further to this the
Oberzensurgericht of the Justice Ministry was made responsible for
cases of recourse to the law made by those affected by a censorship
decision, such as a publisher financially damaged by a censorship case.
But, as Reisner writes, the institution of the Oberzensurgericht did not
in practice serve to liberalise the situation in Prussia, and the arbitrary
nature of decisions made by the censor remained unchecked. The
concept of Volkszensur, suggested in Joseph II's reforms, was not
represented in the Oberzensurgericht. Recourse to the law was to the
authorities of the state, and not to a jury taken from its citizens. The
suggestion, made by Herbert Müllenbach in 1935,[7] that the transformation of the college of censors into a judiciary represented a step
towards the transformation of the *Polizeistaat* into a *Rechtsstaat*,
cannot be taken seriously in view of the increased prosecution of
writers following the tightening of censorship control in 1843. The
idea of the Rechtsstaat, at least in Welcker's liberal sense,[8] implied
moreover, a consistency and reasonableness of action which did not
characterise Friedrich Wilhelm IV's actions in 1843-4 in revoking his
earlier reforms. In fact the transference of the function of the
Oberzensurkollegium to the Oberzensurgericht in July 1843 not only
accompanied the tightening of censorship laws and their enforcement,
but led to a new form of *Index Librorum Prohibitorum*. H.H. Houben
writes,[9] that a type of index of forbidden books had been instituted
by order of Friedrich Wilhelm III in April 1834. But in the early 1840s
during Friedrich Wilhelm IV's partial thaw of censorship control, the
index lapsed. When the monarch asked to see the last quarter's report
of the forbidden books on 7 January 1843 the only one listed was one
published by Edgar Bauer. When, however, the Oberzensurgericht
took over the control of censorship it reinstituted this list in the form
of instructions to the public, and especially to book traders, which told
them – as had the index earlier – what was permitted to be read and
what was forbidden.

Notes

1. Ulla Otto, *Die literarische Zensur als Problem der Soziologie der Politik*,
Stuttgart, 1968, p. 36.
2. Leslie Bodi, *Tauwetter in Wien*, Frankfurt-am-Main, 1977, deals with this
area. The word 'thaw' is used in the sense given it by Ilya Ehrenburg in his novel

Ottepel of 1954, to describe a relaxation in controls such as censorship. The despotic character of Friedrich's enlightened attitude to censorship is expressed in his statement that the people should be allowed to complain, but that they should also obey.

3. Otto, p. 39. See also Franz Schneider, *Pressefreiheit und politische Öffentlichkeit*, Neuwied, 1966, p. 133, who quotes this from Oswald Krempel's 1921 thesis (Cologne) on censorship in the Rhenish press between 1814 and 1848.

4. Otto.

5. See Otto, p. 125, on Sonnenfels. Joseph von Sonnenfels had also banned the popular *Hanswurst* comedy from the Viennese stage in 1770.

6. Hanns-Peter Reisner, *Literatur unter der Zensur. Die politische Lyrik des Vormärz*, Stuttgart, 1975, pp. 44-5.

7. Herbert Müllenbach's thesis, *Die Entwicklung der Pressfreiheit in Preußen, insbesondere in der Rheinprovinz*, Freiburg, 1935.

8. Leonard Krieger, 'The Doctrine of the *Rechtsstaat*', *The German Idea of Freedom*, Chicago, 1972, p. 255, writes, that Welcker wrote in 1813 that the *Rechtsstaat* embodied Reason, and, as far as the determination of rights went, made its laws on the basis of common consent. The development of the idea of the *Rechtsstaat* in Germany owed much to Kant, who wrote in *Theorie und Praxis*, translated in Reiss (ed.), *Kant's Political Writings*, Cambridge, 1970:

> The civil state, regarded purely as a lawful state, is based on the following *a priori* principles:
> 1) the freedom of every member of society as a human being
> 2) the quality of each with all the others as a subject
> 3) the independence of each member of a commonwealth as a citizen.

9. H.H. Houben, *Verbotene Literatur*, Hildesheim, 1965, vol. 1, p. 458.

1.2 CENSORSHIP FROM 1819 IN GERMANY AND MARX'S REACTIONS

Regional differences must be taken into account in describing the type of censorship used in early nineteenth-century Germany. Yet Ute Radlik has also shown,[1] that the censor had been given control over moral as well as political utterances by Metternich, and further argues that this had given censorship a certain 'universal' power over both readers and writers, which the political Napoleonic censor, despite Napoleonic attempts to reduce particularist differences in Germany, had not had. Marx himself comments on this in 1842[2] when he writes that the nineteenth-century censor not only had control over the individual citizen as did the Roman censor, but over the 'öffentlicher Geist' (the 'public spirit') of society. The function of censor as the guardian of morals is revived in the Metternich era, and given a rigour which guards against an easy return to the thaw seen in the 1780s. Like the eighteenth-century absolutist states the restoration monarchies did also include writers amongst their censors, internalising both art and criticism together in the body politic. But though it rarely met, the college of censors had, before 1843, also acted as a further controlling power over these censors, censoring them when their decisions were not acceptable.

It is also necessary to study the particular acts and decrees of the restoration censors to gauge the degree of liberalisation allowed to them by Metternich, and the extent of his power over the various German states and free-cities. Thus a relative liberalisation of the censorship laws in Bavaria in 1818 was revoked by the more 'universal' Carlsbad Decrees of 1819 which followed student activities at the Wartburg Festival of 1817 and the murder of the writer Kotzebue as a Russian spy by the *Burschenschaftler* Karl Sand. With the decrees of 1819 the *Vorzensur*, or pre-censorship of works under 320 pages (or 20 publisher's sheets) was enforced, together with stricter control over political comment on throne and altar. And although the decrees were originally to run for only five years, in 1824 they were extended indefinitely.[3] Heine's *Buch der Lieder* (after which Marx named one of his volumes of verse in 1836) was written under these circumstances. Though, as Heine later wrote, certain towns such as Leipzig and Stuttgart still allowed some liberal interpretations of the decrees, and publishers such as Campe in the free-city of Hamburg would sometimes take the risk of publishing works which might be confiscated in other cities after publication by the *Nachzensur*, the general effect of these censorship decrees was to create a process of 'self-censorship' in the writer which must also be taken into account when reading suppressed subjects through or in the 'silences' in texts written at that time.

In 1830, 1831 and 1832[4] the Carlsbad Decrees of 1819 were again renewed, as a reaction of the government to the July Revolution and its German echoes. Again regional differences also existed, but the effect of these decrees in encouraging 'self-censorship' in the writer must be assumed to have been general. Yet the tightening of the censorship laws saw, apart from the growth of covert metaphoric and ironic modes of expression, a radicalisation in the journals and other writings of the group of writers (including Heine, Gutzkow, Mundt, and Wienbarg) who, in 1835, were made the subject of a ban by the Federal Diet. This followed a general tightening of censorship control from Vienna in June 1834, after which even works of 320 pages were, in some places, subjected to pre-censorship. In 1835 the writers of Young Germany were condemned for publishing attacks on the Christian religion, society and morals, in 'belletristic writings available to all classes'. No mention was made of their criticism of political issues, or of the censorship itself,[5] but this 'silence' could be seen as the government's tactical avoidance of repeating, and giving more publicity than necessary to those attacks on issues which were tacitly known to be out-of-bounds to satire and criticism. Silence, as can be seen from this example, was the weapon of the censor as well as his goal.

Following the ban on the Young Germans of 1835, the Prussian College of Censors issued a condemnation of Heine's 'particularly dangerous' combination of blasphemy with Saint-Simonian sensualism. The writings of Saint Simon, and their translation into German letters by the Young Germans, had been a particularly sharp thorn in the side of Wolfgang Menzel, a critic who often outdid the censor in his enthusiastic protection of Germany's morals against both Young Germans and Young Hegelians. Menzel has also included the poet Chamisso in one of his diatribes,[6] and this is particularly interesting in view of the fact that Chamisso was the editor chosen by Marx — without success — to publish his poetry in 1837. As Marx writes to his father in November 1837, Chamisso had told him that the journal to which he had submitted some of his works had already been made up. It is of particular interest for the purpose of the present discussion, that

Chamisso was moreover in 1837 out of favour with the Prussian
authorities. For although known to many as a Romantic, Chamisso,
inspired by the July Revolution, had in the 1830s taken up the
defence of liberal views which also extended to criticism of the
situation in Prussia. In 1835-6 he had written an essay entitled
'Über Censur und Pressfreiheit', taking up the late eighteenth-century
argument for reforming censorship: the Jacobin Rebmann's similarly
titled essay 'Censur oder Pressfreiheit' (1796) was republished in 1847.
Shortly before his death in 1838 Chamisso also published a collection
of songs by Béranger, the poet from who Marx quotes in 1842 in his
attack on Prussian censorship in the articles on the 'Debates on Press-
Freedom'. In the *Romantische Schule* (one of his works banned after
1835) Heine had written of Chamisso:

> obgleich Zeitgenosse der romantischen Schule, an deren Bewegungen
> er teilnahm, hat doch das Herz dieses Mannes sich in der letzten
> Zeit so wunderbar verjüngt, dass er in ganz neue Tonarten
> überging, sich als einen der eigentümlichsten und bedeutendsten
> modernen Dichter gelten machte und weit mehr dem jungen als
> dem alten Deutschland angehört . . .

> (although a contemporary of the Romantic School, in whose
> movements he took part, the heart of this man has rejuvenated
> itself so wonderfully in recent times, that he has developed quite
> new tones, made himself count as one of the most individual and
> important of modern poets and belongs far more to the Young than
> to the Old Germany . . .)

Houben writes,[7] that Chamisso had in his essay on censorship and
the freedom of the press (referred to previously), praised the Young
German writers, and also defended a form of *Volkszensur*, which
would use a jury representing the 'public conscience' to make decisions
on the banning of a book or on the prosecution of a writer. Chamisso's
views on censorship appear largely to have been influenced by
eighteenth-century Enlightenment views, but his action in defending
the Young German writers in 1835, at the time of the decree banning
their works, was both modern and courageous.

The 1830s saw no relaxation of the censorship regulations of any
real consequence. Only in 1840, with the accession of Friedrich
Wilhelm IV to the throne, did the writers of the liberal opposition to
the Restoration take some hope that the press laws would be liberalised.

Köppen's *Friedrich der Grosse und seine Widersacher* (*Frederick the Great and his Opponents*), which he dedicated to his friend Marx in 1840, took Frederick as a model for the liberal monarch, by naming him as a force of opposition to the Christian-German reaction to rationalism. In defending Frederick, Köppen was both following Hegel and attacking critics of the Enlightenment such as the Romantic Novalis, who had argued in his essay 'Die Christenheit oder Europa' that both the Reformation and Frederick the Great had destroyed the unity of the Holy Roman Empire. Novalis's attack on Frederick was of a very different kind from that of the *Aufklärer* Lessing whom Marx defends in 1842 against the Romantics in one of his essays on censorship. Both Herder and Lessing had criticised the despotic element in Frederick's Enlightenment, while Novalis had attacked it, together with the Revolution of 1789, in the essay 'Glauben und Liebe' of 1798 (written for Friedrich Wilhelm III) as leading to the disintegration of the organic Christian state.

While Köppen's Frederick biography, and other such works, go to explain both the optimism of the liberals in 1840 that Friedrich Wilhelm IV would revive the Prussian Enlightenment, and Friedrich Wilhelm's own desire to play out the role of Frederick the Great, Köppen's idealised radicalisation of Frederick also explains something of why expectations on both sides were disappointed. On 10 August 1840 Friedrich Wilhelm had given an amnesty for all political criminals. On 24 December 1841 (Christmas Eve, so this was a Christian as well as an 'enlightened' action; but the date was also, in pagan mythology, the time of the saturnalia in which the order of society is *temporarily* reversed!) the monarch issued the decrees reforming the censorship regulations in Prussia which Marx was to attack in his article of February 1842 and which Engels also commented on (independently of Marx) in June 1842.[8] This 'liberalisation' had, however, been preceded by other more repressive particular measures, such as the ban on the publishing house of Hoffmann and Campe on 8 December 1841. The apparent thaw of 24 December 1841, which allowed liberal papers such as the *Rheinische Zeitung* and the *Deutsche Jahrbücher* to be published, was followed by a new 'freeze' in 1843, in which bans were placed on publishers, authors, and the journals as such. Both the press and the book trade had expanded greatly in the 1840s and the 'enlightened' monarch of that age, Friedrich Wilhelm IV, found a press very much stronger and more wilful than that supported by Frederick the Great in the 1780s; his liberalisation of the press laws proved, in consequence, to be temporary and brief. One writer deceived by

Friedrich Wilhelm's apparent liberality in 1841 was the poet Georg
Herwegh, who – according to contemporary accounts, and to Heine
in his satirical poem 'Die Audienz' – had dared to ask the King for
further *Geistesfreiheit* in his audience in 1842. Here an interesting
historical parallel appears between Friedrich Wilhelm IV and Joseph II's
successor on the Habsburg throne after Leopold, Francis I. For
Herwegh's interview ended not only with the refusal of his request
for more freedom of speech but with his expulsion from Prussia. As
Francis I had misused Joseph II's liberalisation of censorship regulations
to 'catch out' those writers considered dangerous or subversive to his
government, by giving them, in the proverbial way, just enough rope
'to hang themselves', so Friedrich Wilhelm now used his own liberal-
ising reforms to clamp down even harder than before on the liberals
who had looked to him for progress. Within the course of just over a
year Friedrich Wilhelm IV played out the roles of both Joseph II and
Francis I, combining both *Wechsel* (revolution) and *Willkür* (despotism),
which for Kant, and other 'enlightened' thinkers, should have remained
in opposition to each other. In *König David*, one of the finest poems
of his collection *Romanzero* of 1852, Heine relates the establishment
of the doctrine of the divine right of kings in the biblical story of
King David to this principle of the Wechsel of Willkür from one member
of a dynasty to another, and to the general oppression of the citizens
of the state. Contemporary political references were not made
explicitly, but censorship of the *Romanzero* in 1852 bore witness to
the relevance of Heine's oblique political comments to the contemporary situation![9] The fact that Heine had not been included in the
amnesty for the Young Germans in 1842 may have contributed to his
cynical warning to other writers such as Herwegh not to be deluded by
the Romantic *Schein* of liberality created by Friedrich Wilhelm IV.
Like Heine, Marx had also not been deluded by the *Scheinliberalität*
of Friedrich Wilhelm IV's press instructions, and wrote at the conclusion of his article of February 1842, that the real 'radical cure' for
censorship would be its abolition: 'Die eigentliche Radicalcur der
Censur wäre ihre Abschaffung; denn das Institut ist schlecht, und die
Institutionen sind mächtiger als die Menschen.'

Ironically, the 'abdication' of the Prussian State in the 1830s in
educating its citizens through its writers made it all the easier for some
Young Hegelians and liberals to see their philosophy and literature as
responsible for the enlightenment of public opinion, and to eschew
political action. But though Bauer in 1841 represents this view
(amongst others) when he argues to Marx that philosophy in Germany

is more interesting than politics, more disillusioned writers — such as
Herwegh in 1842 — began to demand a new form of 'party literature'.
Thus, though literature becomes again the responsibility of the
individual writer, the failure of the Enlightenment programme for
reform through controlling writing leads also to the writer's recognition that the centre of power was not cultural but political. Heine's
attack on the assumption made in the Goethean *Kunstperiode*, that
the reverse was the case, is taken up again in a more militant
programme for making literature serve politics by the *Tendenzdichter*
of the 1840s. Here Heine disagreed, however, with the methods of the
radical poets for winning more liberty. Just as he mocked Herwegh's
naive request of the King for more freedom of thought as counter-
productive (the result being more cautionary restrictions on his and
other writers' freedom), so Heine warned the Tendenzdichter that
their attacks on censorship and on the monarchy as such would not
only fail to win more freedom of speech, but would eliminate the
right to speech altogether.

This had been brought home to Heine by the ban placed on his
publisher Campe on 8 December 1841, after the publication of some
political verse by the Tendenzdichter Dingelstedt. Heine had also
blamed Hoffmann von Fallersleben for this ban,[10] arguing that the
radicalism of the Tendenzdichter was leading to the silencing of all
writers. Mocking Dingelstedt's naivete in his *Zeitgedicht* entitled
Bei des Nachtwächters Ankunft zu Paris, Heine wrote:

> Und wird uns der ganze Verlag verboten,
> So schwindet am Ende von selbst die Zensur.

> (And if our whole publishing house is banned
> Then censorship will disappear on its command.)

Heine is of course being highly ironic — arguing that when Tendenzdichter like Dingelstedt succeed in closing down all the publishing
houses open to liberal writers with their radical writings then censorship will fade away for lack of literature to censor. Heine is also
arguing here that the censor is dependent upon the writer for his
existence, while the writer need not be dependent on the censor, or
risk the liberty he has by making his art the victim of the system from
which he would escape.

Literary wit had represented intelligence, and even a form of
genius for the eighteenth-century Rationalists, but the nineteenth-

century censor, though sometimes a writer himself, must in practice often have appeared to embody the opposite of wit as well as of freedom of speech. One story of a Prussian censor, retold by Nicolaevsky,[11] goes that the censor, with whom Marx was later to battle when editor of the *Rheinische Zeitung*, 'suppressed an advertisement of a translation of Dante's *Divine Comedy* by "Philalethes", the later King John of Saxony, with the comment that "No comedy should be made of 'divine things' " '. Thus, while irony and metaphor might sometimes enable the writer to smuggle criticism past his authorities, it – like any of his more direct statements – was also in danger of being misunderstood and cut by an overly suspicious, or ignorant, censor.

According to Mehring in his 1918 biography of Marx (*Karl Marx. The Story of his Life*, London, 1966, p. 44) it had in fact been the issue of censorship which had turned the Berlin Hegelian Club into *Die Freien* and led them to take an interest in political issues as well as in philosophical problems. Certainly a consequence of Friedrich Wilhelm IV's tightening of censorship restrictions in 1842 and 1843 was the politicisation of literature and the realisation by many writers of the restrictive effects of censorship. Yet this politicisation was to some extent kept within the limits of Idealist philosophy, and, by the censor, within the limits of such 'underground languages' as irony and parody.

Marx expresses his contemporaries' dissatisfaction with the interference of the censor in the publication of literary works in, as we have seen, condemning the effect of the censor's 'writing over' of another's work as the creation of hypocrisy in writing. Yet another form of such 'hypocrisy' was, of course, irony, the tool used by those wanting to escape the censor. This awareness of hypocrisy and ambiguity in the text, the awareness of the text as 'palimpsest' as Heine once put it, led not only to the use of ambiguity by liberal writers wanting to 'smuggle'[12] their ideas past the censor, but – as in the case of Heine and (later) Young Hegelians such as Bauer – to the distinction between the esoteric and exoteric levels of meaning in a text by means of which the conservative, 'exoteric' Hegel was reinterpreted as the revolutionary 'esoteric' critic of the Prussian State.[13]

In the new press censorship instruction of 1841, as Marx commented in February 1842, responsibility for the pre-censorship of journals was taken from editors and publishers and given to the censor. Yet both prior to and following that decree, publishers, authors, and editors had all to impose censorship upon themselves in deciding what could be smuggled past the censor. The threat of a ban being placed on publishing houses and journals placed editors and publishers into the dual roles of avoiding censorship and acting as censors themselves. It is therefore not surprising to see Marx acting in the role of 'censor' as editor of the *Rheinische Zeitung* of 1843, but also enjoying the results of his achievements in smuggling articles past the official censor and seeing him and his successor corrected and dismissed by his superiors, before the paper was finally banned in 1843 by the order of Friedrich Wilhelm IV himself.

Two of Marx's prime concerns as both writer and editor in 1842-3 were excellence of style and the freedom of expression. In his article of 1842 on the 'Debates in Parliament on the Freedom of the Press' Marx argued his case against censorship and for the freedom of the press by turning Herder's thesis that poetry was the *Ursprache*, or original language, of the people into the statement that every people expresses its spirit in its press. Hegel, too, as Shlomo Avineri has shown, made use of Herder's concept of the *Volksgeist* in his theory of the state.[14] Marx's substitution of 'press' for 'poetry' in his statement, 'jedes Volk spricht seinen Geist in seiner Presse aus', not only suggests that the state should regard the press as voicing its own spirit, but, in rewriting Romantic phraseology, is also symptomatic of his growing rejection of 'Romantic' elements in Friedrich Wilhelm IV's Prussia — his ultramontanist policies and opposition to reason.[14] Marx's variation on Herder's phrase is also characteristic of the imaginative way in which he is to continue using the poetry of his past, and parody, for philosophical and political argument.

The Young Hegelian Marx appeared to share Heine's Hegelian belief, expressed in 1834 in his *Zur Geschichte der Religion und Philosophie in Deutschland*, that progress was to be dated in the modern world from the Reformation and, in particular, from the establishment of freedom of thought and the discovery of the printing-press. And it was in his articles written against censorship that Marx both practised and expressed the belief in freedom of speech silent in his poetry of 1836-7. Both Heine and Marx in their journalistic work extended the Enlightenment belief in the civilising function of literature to a defence of the press, but the censorship of such defences in the 1830s and 1840s also led Marx to condemn censorship as a hypocritical rather than as an enlightened institution.

The ban placed on the Young Germans in 1835 had explicitly condemned them for writing 'belletristic' articles available to 'all classes' of the people. This was the danger of the press in the nineteenth century: the threat of unification of society from below, or through such instruments as the popular press, was seen by the Prussian state as unbalancing the careful balance of monarchic, state, and particularist powers. In 1844 Heine mocked the use of the censor to create a substitute and fictional form of intellectual unity pointing out that this unity was based on uniformity of thought as well as silence.[16] The tightening of censorship restrictions in the 1840s, from which Heine and other writers suffered, was indeed a reaction to the growing power of the popular press. It showed too that literature was no longer the province of a few *esprits* but of the many, and Friedrich Wilhelm IV's transformation of his role from eighteenth-century enlightened ruler to Romantic ultramontanist can (as claimed earlier) be seen in this context as his recognition of the changed conditions which made the manipulation of enlightened censorship reform too dangerous in the context of the nineteenth century.

Marx's claim in 1842 that the *Volksgeist* was expressed in the press, rather than through the institutions of the state, repudiated both the Prussian monarch's claim that the state was representative of the spirit of its citizens and his right to censor the press.[17] Censorship was, in Marx's terms, as an attack on the *Volksgeist*, the state's attempt to silence itself – a contradictory and irrational action. Marx shows how the censor has thus created a *verkehrte Welt* (a topsy-turvy world) for himself, in which his attempts at enlightenment must always turn into their opposites.

When attacking the censor for making good style and honesty in writing impossible, in his 'Comments on the Latest Prussian Censorship Instruction' in February 1842, Marx had himself upheld the eighteenth-century ideal – expressed in Buffon's dictum 'le style c'est l'homme même' – of the integrity of the writer. Marx's attack on the censor for creating hypocrisy in writing by forcing the writer to write in a style not his own, or by actually writing over, or cutting down another's work, was also related to his Young Hegelian belief in the role of self-consciousness in the realisation of Reason and the concept of Freedom in history. A writer's style was necessary to his consciousness of his self,[18] and Marx went so far as to argue that the censor was performing an act of theft in taking away the style of a writer, for this form was his property (*Eigentum*) and his spiritual individuality (*geistige Individualität*). By acting as a thief the state is again shown to be performing the opposite function to the one it has set itself as the guardian ('census-taker') of property and morals. In his 'Comments on the Latest Prussian Censorship Instruction' Marx also shows that the document is contradictory and hypocritical in, for example, encouraging official criticism to condemn unofficial criticism. In showing that, in these and other ways, the hypocrisy of the censor has resulted in a *verkehrte*, topsy-turvy liberalisation of censorship, Marx also ironically shows Friedrich Wilhelm IV's 'saturnalian' liberation of writers from the restrictions of censoring on Christmas Eve 1841 to have been a parody of itself; for it has not turned authority but liberty on to its head, resulting in more repressive rather than more liberal measures. But Marx also inverts the state's idea of itself as an institution which, representing reason, must confer its identity upon its citizens, by implying that its use of the censor has only succeeded in taking away the writer's identity, and that of the *Volksgeist*, expressed through him.

Marx's own use of older, Romantic models in his early poetry, to express himself about his own and others experiences, may also, in view of his awareness of the censorship of more current liberal writers, be taken as an example of 'writing over' a text with a style other than the author's own. Buffon's phrase, 'le style c'est l'homme même' can be traced back to antiquity, and to the idea of 'hominibus fuit oratio qualis uita', as discussed in Seneca, *Epistle 11, 4*.[19] From this concept of poetry as the expression of the self (to which tradition Herder's statement on the spirit of the people expressed in poetry also belongs), the satirist Aristophanes was able to turn writers into the tropes which best caricatured their failings.[20] It is not too long a step from here to Heine's suggestion that history could also express itself in literary terms as tragedy or farce, or to Marx's idea in the *Eighteenth Brumaire* of 1852. Marx's caricature of Napoleon III as a parody of Napoleon I not only satirises the coup of 1851 as a parodistic repetition of history, but the spirit of Napoleon III's empire as farce. In 1842, Marx, as we have just seen, has already accused the censor of creating a parodistic 'verkehrte Welt' (a topsy-turvy world) in Germany, by destroying the spirit of its people as expressed in its writings which the state itself was to represent. As the censor is shown to be creating criminality and hypocrisy in style, so too the censor comes to embody these vices himself.

Parody is thus not merely a literary means of escaping the censor for Marx but a metaphoric way of caricaturing him. The problems associated with the use of parody in Marx's work will be returned to in Part Two of this study. There it will, for instance, be argued that continued use of parody and irony came to restrict Marx and other Young Hegelians to the same topics and to a coterie audience: thus not only history but parody itself comes to repeat itself as farce! Looking

back to 1828-30 when he had written his Italian *Reisebilder*, Heine
wrote in 1853, in the conclusion of the *II. Préface de la dernière
édition des Reisebilder*,[21] that the censor had created the 'fear before
one's own words', the trivialisation of literature, and encouraged the
obscurity of scientific and secret languages. All of these problems are
relevant to an understanding of Marx's early works, of the relationship
between his use of parody and the threat of censorship, and of the
centrality of the subject of writing itself to his juvenilia.

Heine's suggestion that the external censor was internalised by the
writer practising self-censorship on his own work also points to another
kind of silence in his works, and in those of his contemporaries. It is
the silence not of passages cut by the censor, though a knowledge of
these is important too in the reading of his texts, but the art of
indicating the importance of something which cannot be said directly
by irony, parody, or metaphor. To read content into the gaps of a
text is a highly speculative undertaking and Althusser's method of
reading texts symptomatically, for instance, raises many theoretical as
well as practical problems.[22] Yet the understanding of an author's
awareness of the workings of self-censorship in a time of external
censorship is also important for an understanding of his own methods
of reading. It was from Heine's awareness of the creation of exoteric
and esoteric levels of meaning in times of censorship that he made
what he called his 'discovery of the secret of the Hegelian school' –
the existence of an esoteric revolutionary Hegel concealed beneath the
apologist of the Prussian State. In order to describe the concealment of
sensualism by the Christian Church, from the Middle Ages to the
nineteenth-century Biedermeier, Heine had also used the image of the
clothing of the Greek gods in Christian garments in art and myth. His
story (in the *Romantische Schule*) of how the mediaeval monks had
covered Venus' nakedness with an apron was taken over by Marx in his
doctoral dissertation of 1841 (giving us an indication of his knowledge
of Heine's banned work). Marx writes that Gassendi had attempted to
reconcile his Catholic conscience with his heathen knowledge and
Epicurus with the Church, but that his action had been as useless as
that of those who had wanted to throw a nun's habit over the
beautiful body of the Greek Laïs. Thus Marx too was conscious, as his
article of February 1842 explicitly shows, of the co-existence of
conflicting meanings and ideologies in texts published in times of
censorship, which could sometimes only later be understood.

Following both Heine's and Marx's example we should also now be
able to put Marx's own early poetic works, written between 1835

and 1837 when the poets of Young Germany were being subject to the most stringent of censorship controls, into their proper context, and interpret their 'silences', or symptoms of silence, as well as their exoteric meaning. Unlike Althusser, whose theories will be returned to briefly later, I shall emphasise the importance of knowing the empirical forms of censorship familiar to the authors involved in our analysis, to an understanding of their use of self-censorship, and the consequent silences in their work.

Notes

1. Ute Radlik, 'Heine in der Zensur der Restaurationsepoche', in J. Hermand and M. Windfuhr (eds.), *Literatur der Restaurationsepoche*, Stuttgart, 1970, p. 460 ff.

2. New MEGA, Berlin, 1975, vol. I/1, p. 98.

3. Hanns Peter Reisner, *Literatur unter der Zensur, Die Politische Lyrik des Vormärz*, Stuttgart, 1975, p. 32. Marx also discusses this in his 'Comments on the Latest Prussian Censorship Instruction', but under cover of the argument that the law was a 'liberal' one which – though extended indefinitely – had not been put into practice before its renewal by the equally 'liberal' (read 'repressive') instruction of December 1841. Marx's purpose is to argue that the ostensibly liberal reform of 1841 was in fact more repressive than 1818.

4. Radlik, p. 462.

5. Reisner, p. 36, points out that 'censorship' was not explicitly mentioned in the Carlsbad Decrees.

6. See *Das Junge Deutschland*, Jost Hermand (ed.), Stuttgart, 1967, p. 336.

7. H.H. Houben, *Verbotene Literatur*, Hildesheim, 1965, vol. 1, p. 103.

8. Published in the *Rheinische Zeitung*, no. 195, 14 July 1842 (anon.).

9. See M. Rose, *Die Parodie. Eine Funktion der biblischen Sprache in Heines Lyrik*, Meisenheim, 1976, p. 76 ff.

10. I have discussed this in ' "Adam der Erste" und das Verlagsverbot vom 8 December 1841', *Heine Jahrbuch*, 1975, pp. 70-6.

11. Boris Nicolaevsky and Otto Maenchen-Helfen, *Karl Marx: Man and Fighter* (1935), Harmondsworth, 1976, p. 33.

12. Walter Hömberg, *Zeitgeist und Ideenschmuggel*, Stuttgart, 1975, p. 32, refers to Gutzkow speaking in 1832 of *Ideenschmuggel* (the smuggling of ideas) as becoming a way of life under the censor. The term was often repeated.

13. Like censorship, the parody used by Young Germans and Young Hegelians could also be described as a way of 'writing over' another's text: yet the old was allowed to shine through the new text in the parody, whereas the censor might obliterate or cut it out altogether in his 'rewriting'.

14. Shlomo Avineri, *Hegel's Theory of the Modern State*, Cambridge, 1972, p. 16.

15. Sidney Hook writes in *From Hegel to Marx* (p. 128) that Arnold Ruge's *Halle Yearbooks* (the *Hallische Jahrbücher* begun in 1838) had launched an attack on Romanticism in literature and politics. Ruge especially condemned ultramontanist tendencies in Friedrich Wilhelm's policies, contrasting them with the free spirit of Prussian protestantism. Ruge followed this campaign with an

attack on the historical school of Law, and, particularly, on Leo and Savigny. (It will be recalled that Marx had heard Savigny lecture in Berlin.) Hook's description of Ruge's attack on Romanticism in the *Halle Yearbook* of 1840 (Hook, p. 134) sounds ironically similar to Mehring's description of the three volumes of Marx's 1836 poems:

> Fairy tales, ghosts, miracles, dreams, night, longing, moonshine – surely these were not the only themes which could be sung. The interests of the profane world, the workaday struggle, the forces liberated by the industrial revolution were just as legitimate subject matter of true poetry as the transcendental longings of the lonely soul.

16.   In Caput II of *Deutschland. Ein Wintermärchen*, the satire referred to by Marx in *The German Ideology*, Heine wrote:

> . . . Die geistige Einheit gibt uns die Zensur,
> Die wahrhaft ideelle –
>
> Sie gibt die innere Einheit uns,
> Die Einheit im Denken und Sinnen;
> Ein einiges Deutschland thut uns not,
> Einig nach aussen und innen.

17.   Here Marx also radicalises Kant's defence of free speech (in *Theorie und Praxis*, Reiss, p. 85) as creating 'a liberal attitude of mind' in the subjects of the state – when also showing 'respect and devotion towards the existing constitution' – and as ensuring the enlightenment of the ruler, who, as representative of 'the general will of the people', must be able to listen to their free voice to fulfil his duties to the state.

18.   See conclusion of Marx's article on the new press instruction of December 1841.

19.   M.H. Abrams, *The Mirror and the Lamp*, New York, 1953, Chap. IX.

20.   Frances Muecke, 'Aristophanes: the Staging of Parody', paper written for the Seminar on Parody held at the Humanities Research Centre, Canberra, in July 1976.

21.   Heinrich Heine, *Historisch-kritische Ausgabe der Werke*, vol. 6, Jost Hermand (ed.), Düsseldorf, 1973, p. 358.

22.   I have discussed this subject in a paper 'Althusser's symptomatic reading method in the light of his "Essays in Self-Criticism" ', given in the History of Ideas Unit, Canberra, in 1977.

2.1 MARX'S POETRY: 'ROMANTIC MOONSHINE'?

Statements, which will be considered again when discussing the 'second censorship' of Marx's poetic attempts in the twentieth century, that Marx's verse belongs to a conservative Romantic tradition, have ignored the censorship which was in force at the time of its composition, as well as the liberal nature of the Romantic models which Marx imitated. Michael Levin, for example, in his article, 'Marxism and Romanticism: Marx's debt to German conservatism' (in *Political Studies*, 1974, pp. 400-13) proposes

(1)   that Marxism derives some of its social perspectives from the conservative and even reactionary thinking that had long been dominant in Germany, and that there are some affinities between Marxism and Romanticism,

and

(2)   that Marxism does not follow simply as a logical development or extension of the radical tradition of the Enlightenment, and the supporters of the French Revolution.

One of Levin's mistakes in applying these premises to Marx himself is to assume (pp. 400-1) that censorship in Germany had prevented any tradition of revolutionary literature, and that Marx had grown up in a society from which social criticism was absent. This, as Heinz Monz and other biographers of Marx have shown, was simply not the case in Trier in the 1830s. One of the first German socialist writers, Ludwig Gall, had published his criticism of conditions of the working classes in 1835 in Trier; and other liberal and radical comments — of which Marx was certainly aware — had drawn the attention of the authorities to that city.

Marx's extant poems, written between 1835 and 1837, and collected in three volumes for his fiancée, Jenny von Westphalen and in one for his father sent to him on the occasion of his birthday in October 1837, are youthful exercises in the art of poetic expression. Born in 1818, Marx was 19 when he decided, as he wrote on 10 November 1837 to his father, to give up his attempts to become a poet.

Johann Hugo von Wyttenbach, headmaster of the Trier Gymnasium which Marx attended from the winter semester of 1830-1 until the summer semester of 1835, was not only a Kantian, but had, in the 1790s, been a Jacobin sympathiser. As Nicolaevsky states,[1] Wyttenbach's revolutionary, liberal sympathies had also involved him in activities in the 1830s such as the Hambach Festival of 1832 and the 1834 banquet held at the Kasino-Gesellschaft to support the constitutional movement. For this and other activities Wyttenbach was finally removed from the Directorship of the Trier Gymnasium in November 1835.

Wyttenbach's sympathetic attitudes to liberal reform represent a not untypical reaction to the changing economic-political conditions in Trier in the early nineteenth century. Nicolaevsky argues, for example, that with increased taxation many in Trier had turned against the French towards the end of the Napoleonic era and that the defeat of Napoleon had been welcomed. Following the Restoration in 1815 Trier was put under Prussian rule. But again, changed economic circumstances preceded a shift in political sympathies. Following the establishment in 1834 of the *Zollverein*, the profits of the Rhenish wine-growers were put in jeopardy, and their taxes again increased. The mid-1830s in Trier thus saw a new sympathy with the French liberal tradition, revived in the July Revolution of 1830. Nicolaevsky writes that 'vintagers from the Moselle area actually took part in the famous Hambacher Fest held by the liberals on 27 May 1832', and that 'In the Rhineland the old francophile tendencies underwent a mighty revival'. Nicolaevsky mentions both a following for Saint-Simonism (condemned by the Archbishop of Trier) and Ludwig Gall's socialism in the 1830s, and other critics have found a Saint-Simonian influence in the ideas of Gall himself. Gall's pamphlet on labour and value, which appeared in Trier in 1835, also coincided with the Frankfurt Diet's ban on Young Germany writers such as Heine and Gutzkow, and its condemnation of Saint-Simonism. It was Marx's future father-in-law, Ludwig von Westphalen who is said to have introduced the young Marx to the ideas of Saint-Simon while Marx was still in Trier, and it is clear that it was a talking-point in the city in the 1830s. The absence of any direct references to it in Marx's poetry, either in that written in Trier or in Berlin, where Marx had also come into contact with Varnhagen von Ense's salon (where Saint-Simonism was also being discussed), is but one of the 'silences' in Marx's texts which is possible to take as a symptom of the self-censorship resulting from the ban on Saint-Simonian and Young German writings at that time.

The demands for constitutional reform put in the Hambach Festival on 27 May 1832 were echoed in Trier in several different ways. Both Marx's father and his headmaster Wyttenbach had taken part in the Kasino-Gesellschaft banquet for the Deputies to the Rhineland Diet on 12 January 1834, which — as Nicolaevsky argues — had been an opportunity to express support for the Diet under the threat of its abolition by the King.[2]

Both Heinrich Marx and Wyttenbach were also members of a group of Kantians,[3] and instilled their Kantian beliefs in the student Marx. A reference to Kant's *Anthropologie* in the letter in which Kant's father attempts to decipher one of his son's poems (MEGA, 1(2), p. 187) leads us back to a work in which poetry is raised above all the arts to the function of developing the human being, the central subject of the *Anthropologie*.[4] Kant had also, however, condemned mediocre verse,[5] the failing in Marx's poetic attempts which his father warns him against in the same letter mentioned above.

Wyttenbach's programme, as he described it in 1834, was the education of young men to the belief in progress, reason, and morals. Reason and free will, Kant and Rousseau, are set up as ideals, while the verses of Schiller, Klopstock, and the Romantics were set for the upper classes of the school to train the imagination as well as the faculties of Reason. Like Kant in his *Anthropologie*, Wyttenbach held poetry to be a proper handmaiden to the study of ethics. The poems collected by Wyttenbach for his volume celebrating the principle of liberty in 1800 contained several works by Schiller (such as the hymn *An die Freude*), and it is clear that from the 1790s, throughout the Restoration to the 1830s, Wyttenbach held up Schiller's verse as an example of liberal literature, to friends and students alike. The *Lesebücher* edited by Wyttenbach in 1825 and 1827 also contained works by Schiller, Goethe, Herder, and others imitated by Marx in his poetry of 1835-7, and represent for Wyttenbach all that was 'gross, edel, und erhaben'.[6] Significantly, Schiller is also described in Heine's *Romantische Schule* (in which he had praised Chamisso as a new 'Young German') as both a great revolutionary and a cosmopolitan:

> Schiller schrieb für die grossen Ideen der Revolution,
> er zerstörte die geistigen Bastillen, er baute an dem
> Tempel der Freiheit, der alle Nationen gleich einer
> einzigen Brüdergemeinde umschliessen soll.[7]

(Schiller wrote for the great ideas of the Revolution, he destroyed the

Bastilles of the spirit, he worked on building the temple of freedom, which would contain all nations as in a single community of men.) The paraphrase of Schiller's *An die Freude*, which Heine gives here, is echoed in Marx's poem *Lucinde*:

> Bruderkuss und Herzenseinigung
>   Schliesset alle in den Kreis,
> Nicht mehr trennen Stand und Meinung,
>   Liebe herrscht und ihr Geheiss.

> (The kiss of brothers and union of hearts
>   Encloses all into a whole,
> Estate and opinion no longer part us,
>   Love and its behest now rule.)

Marx's sympathy for Schiller is, as we have seen, both based in the Kantian education given him by his father and Wyttenbach, and (in view, for example, of the similar defence of Schiller given by Heine) modern. Marx's imitation of what have been termed older Romantic models can be placed into a tradition of eighteenth-century Enlightenment liberal thinking. But, in that those traditions were also taken as authority by liberals of the 1830s — from Wyttenbach to Heine[8] — we may also take the eighteenth-century tradition to be acting as a 'stand-in' for contemporary liberal models such as the Young German school when those were banned. More explicit reference to Heine and Saint-Simonian sensualism in the fragments of a comic novel, entitled *Scorpion und Felix*, attached to the volume of poetry of 1837 make Marx's awareness of these models clear. Another later clue to this is Marx's 1843 defence of Lessing — some of whose works were also banned in the Decree of 1835 — in one of his attacks on the censor (MEGA, I/1 (i), p. 225).

Heinz Monz has also told us[9] that Wyttenbach's speech for the departure of the senior students in 1835 was on the theme of the battle between the Ancients and the Moderns, and that Marx would then have heard Wyttenbach argue that a balance should be kept between the two. In Marx's poetry, this balance was often between the exoteric and esoteric imagery of the text — where the ancient image (as Prometheus or Icarus in Marx's 1837 poems) would serve to express the essence of the modern situation which could not — for aesthetic or political reasons — be spoken of directly. Marx's use of the figures of Prometheus and Icarus as personae in his poems of 1836-7 both distances himself from the words of the text and points to this ambivalence in his work, in which contemporary and personal messages are masked by fictions borrowed from ancient or classical authors. The frequent use of parenthesis in Marx's poetry is an indication of the fear of direct expression and a means of saying things which otherwise — for personal or broader social reasons — had to be kept silent.

In 1832 Wyttenbach was placed under police review for activities relating to the Hambach festival, where German liberals and republicans had gathered to celebrate the ideals of the 1830 Revolutions. From 1832 to 1834 he had also let a *junges deutsches literarisches Kränzchen*, consisting of students and teachers of the Gymnasium, meet near the school. The name of the group suggests ties with the *junges Deutschland*, the Young Germany banned in 1835 for, amongst other things, importing the Saint-Simonism also banned by the Archbishop of Trier.

Nicolaevsky claims[10] that Wyttenbach's Gymnasium was under police surveillance from 1830. Though at this time police control was in general tight, following the revolutions of 1830 and the constitutional movement in the south of Germany, the Trier school had indeed come to be known for both its lack of discipline and liberal activities. Finally, one boy was arrested in 1834 for writing political poems, and others were named to the authorities. Monz writes[11] that the literary *Kränzchen*, or circle, had also been grouped around the poet Eduard Duller, who had been forced to leave Vienna because of difficulties with the censorship, and another poet Friedrich von Sallet, who had got into difficulties with the authorities for some satires he had written. Although it is not clear if Marx was personally associated in any way with this group, it is a sign of the awareness which existed within the Gymnasium of current political issues and of censorship, as well as of the Young German writers banned in 1835. The apparent absence of any reference to the work of this group in Marx's own poetry of 1835-7 must be considered in the light of what we know about the Trier Gymnasium and its students. Wyttenbach's interest in the works of liberal writers and his awareness of the censorship of them by past and present authorities must also not be ignored in assessing Marx's knowledge of the Young Germany and his silence on that subject.

When it is known that the *Poetenklub* which Marx joined in Bonn (with the poets Emanuel Geibel and Karl Grün) was also thought — according to the police records of 1834-5 — to have engaged in some 'revolutionary' activities,[12] then it may seem even stranger that there is so little explicit reference to contemporary liberal or radical poetry in

Marx's verse. Very little discussion of this 'silence' in Marx's work has yet taken place, and critics have not minded avoiding it in summing up Marx's early poetic works as conventional and Romantic. This latter view, however, gives us little more than an exoteric reading of the poetry, based, moreover, on a broad generalisation about the historical character of Marx's models; for not all literary historians would call Schiller a Romantic, and none would categorise Ovid — whose *Tristia* Marx translates — as such. Marx's own designation of his poetic works as 'Romantic moonshine', which, we have suggested, is followed by a second case of silencing the works' more liberal character, cannot be taken as the last word on the subject. Marx's denigration of his poetry, in the letter in which he also announces his 'conversion' to Hegel, is a 'liberating' moment in which he breaks from the past those works represent: from Kant, the classical image, his youth, and the art of speaking indirectly about reality. In breaking from these things Marx, as will be seen in *Scorpion und Felix*, also begins to speak openly of the liberal, modern tradition concealed behind the classical and the Romantic, and, later, of a cause for this concealment, the censor himself.

It was during the years 1835-7 that Marx wrote the poetic works now published in the new edition of the MEGA in 1975. One of these volumes of 1836 is entitled *Buch der Lieder* after Heine's first collection of verse, and Heine's Preface written for the second edition of his book in spring 1837 could just as well serve as a motto for Marx's volume:

> . . . Ertse Gedichte! Sie müssen auf nachlässigen, verblichenen Blättern geschrieben sein, dazwischen, hier und da, müssen welke Blumen liegen, oder eine blonde Locke . . .

> (. . . First poems! They must be written on untidy, faded pages, in between, here and there, limp flowers should be lying, or a blond lock . . .)

Yet Heine's Preface again refers to the 'rejuvenation' of Chamisso (that is, to Chamisso's role as a Young German) and alludes to Heine's fight for the principle of freedom in his writings since the *Buch der Lieder* of 1827. 1837 was a year in which Heine saw some of the strictest censorship practised on his works. The re-editing of his 'safer' love poems of 1827 at this time of increased censorship also reminds us that the *Buch der Lieder* was itself published under the shadow of the Carlsbad Decrees, renewed, as we have seen, in 1825. This irony can surely not have escaped Heine and we find in his works of the 1830s several references to the need to choose between the alternatives of love poetry and revolutionary verse, and to how the revolutionary must sometimes be painted over in lighter tones by the other. Though for Heine, the Saint-Simonian, sensualism was yet another side of the philosophy of liberty, it had traditionally served as an alternative to political statement in the more conservative literary tradition of the Biedermeier, and to use it thus was for Heine a necessary but not entirely satisfactory way of quietly mocking those traditions.

To repeat the love poetry of his youth in 1837 was also to comment on the retrograde movement of history under the Restoration. And Marx's imitation of Heine in 1837, though appropriate to his first youthful love poems, is also symptomatic of the repetition of the historical conditions under which Heine had written his verses in 1827, of, that is, increased censorship.[13] Marx's poetry demonstrates the immediate effect of the censorship of the Young Germans in 1835, in its self-censoring silences and choice of older 'Romantic' models. But, in imitating works of Young Germans such as Heine and Chamisso, which had, in their earlier period, been made politically 'safe' by the Carlsbad Decrees of 1819, it also contains an indirect reference to the continuing power of the censor in the Restoration. Like other writers of the *Sturm und Drang* and like the Young Germans of the 1830s who saw themselves as a second 'Storm and Stress', the young Schiller had also been censored and it is, significantly, one of these works of the *Sturm und Drang*, the drama *Die Räuber*, which Marx imitates in his drama *Oulanem*. Schiller's *Xenion* entitled *Visitator* (of 1796) ironically compares the function of the customs inspector to that of the censor (referring too to the German fear of the Jacobin coming out of France) as Heine was to do in his satire, *Deutschland. Ein Wintermärchen* in 1844:

Öffnet die Coffers. Ihr habt doch nichts contrebandes geladen?
Gegen die Kirche? den Staat? Nichts von französischem Gut?

(Open the cases! You aren't carrying anything contraband?
Contra the Church? the State? Nothing of French origin?)

Marx's use of early works by authors censored when he was writing in 1835 also of course serves to mention these writers without imitating their more dangerous writings. Only later, however, does Marx (with

other Young Hegelians) master the art of the Young Germans'
Zensurstil, or 'Aesopian' language.

Explicit references to censorship, as in Schiller's *Xenion*, are few
in Marx's work. Yet it may be significant that Marx twice takes up the
opening of Ovid's *Tristia* in the volume of poetic works for his father in
1837. While the translation given in the poems is little more than a
rewriting of Ovid's story of the exiled poet who sends his book out in
his stead, the paraphrase given in *Scorpion und Felix* of Book II of the
Tristia omits some verses, but adds Ovid's comments on the political
reasons for his exile which the poetic translation of Book I had not
given. As we shall see, *Scorpion und Felix* contains several allusions to
contemporary events and to the writers of the Young Germany not
made in the poems and, in many ways, appears to serve Marx in bringing
to the surface the concealed models of his youth at the same time as it
frees him from them and from those openly imitated in the poems.
Later, in his February 1842 article on the new censorship instruction,
Marx calls on Goethe, Schiller and Sterne's *Tristram Shandy* as
authorities for his arguments against censorship, providing a further
clue to a continuity in his use of those writers in his early work as
upholders of enlightened principles antipathetic to censorship.

Apart from calling on Schiller and Goethe to serve as authorities for
his argument, Marx had also referred to the rationalist Voltaire in his
'Comments on the Latest Prussian Censorship Instruction', quoting from
L'enfant prodigue. Von Westphalen had encouraged the young Marx
in his reading of Voltaire as well as of Homer and Shakespeare. And
that great French rationalist had, like Montesquieu, taught the art of
'idea-smuggling' to others through his *Philosophical Letters* and other
works. Like Montesquieu in his *Persian Letters* Voltaire had used
subterfuge and metaphor to speak of contemporary events through
other spatially or temporally distant images. China, for instance, as
Heine's satire on Friedrich Wilhelm IV as the 'Kaiser von China' shows,
was a well-known metaphor for the Prussian State, referring to parallels
between China and Pufendorf's bureaucratic system as well as to the
monarch's autocratic character. Thus Marx's description of Article II
of the Instruction (forbidding any praise of revolutionary forces in
other countries) as preventing 'not only any frank discussion of Prussian
affairs, but not even of Chinese affairs . . .'[14] may imply that China be
read 'esoterically' as a synonym for Prussia. If this is so the sentence is
tautologically saying, that Prussia is preventing frank discussion of
Prussian as well as the esoteric criticism of 'Chinese' (Prussian) affairs.
Marx indicates by his choice of China as the country censored by

Article II that the aim of that instruction is related rather to internal security than to concern for the affairs of foreign countries and that the Prussian censor, aware of the satiric substitution of China for Prussia, will now also have legal support for any elimination of such passages. Reference to this 'cat-and-mouse' game of the censor with the satirist and to the latter's need to use metaphor and irony points also, however, to the fact that there had been little or no so-called 'frank discussion of Prussian ideas' to be forbidden.

In this and other essays in 1842-3, Marx not only speaks of the way in which the censor creates irony and hypocrisy in literature by 'writing over' the work of another writer, or by causing that writer to conceal his real thoughts under the cover of metaphor, but himself uses irony to illustrate this point and, under threat of censorship, to practise that art. Such use of irony and parody enabled Marx to make statements otherwise forbidden, but also created 'silences' in the texts — not 'visible' to all readers — which were also to limit the communication and effectiveness of his statements. Marx's concealment of his knowledge of contemporary political events and philosophical developments in his poetic works of the 1830s is an earlier, but similar (if more extreme) case of self-censorship which leads to the substitution of accepted images and figures for those censored or disapproved of by authority.

Notes

1.   Boris Nicolaevsky and Otto Maenchen-Helfen, *Karl Marx: Man and Fighter*, Harmondsworth, 1976, Ch. 1.

2.   Nicolaevsky, pp. 10-11.

3.   Ibid., p. 13.

4.   I. Kant, *Anthropologie*, Fr. und Leipzig, 1799, p. 210.

5.   Ibid., p. 212.

6.   Heinz Monz, *Karl Marx — Grundlagen der Entwicklung zu Leben und Werk*, 2nd edn. of *Karl Marx und Trier*, Trier, 1973, p. 146 ff. Monz also mentions that Schiller's son, Ernst von Schiller, was *Landsgerichtsrat* in Trier in the 1820s.

7.   Heinrich Heine, *Sämtliche Werke*, E. Elster (ed.), Leipzig, 1893, vol. 5, p. 253.

8.   The young Friedrich Engels wrote to Friedrich Graeber on 30 July 1839, that it was now generally accepted (amongst Young Germans) that Schiller was Germany's 'greatest liberal poet'. But in view of the continuing censorship of living liberal poets this might also be seen as an ironic reference to the absence of competition resulting from the censor's actions.

9.   Monz, p. 166.

10.   Nicolaevsky, p. 14.

11.   Monz, p. 175.

12.   Nicolaevsky, p. 19.

13.   Katharina Mommsen has also touched on this subject in her article, 'Heines lyrische Anfänge in Schatten der Karlsbader Beschlüsse', in *Wissen aus Erfahrungen*, Alexander von Bormann (ed.), Tübingen, 1976.

14.   *Marx/Engels' Collected Works*, vol. 1, p. 115.

2.2 SYMPTOMS OF CENSORSHIP IN MARX'S POETIC WORKS

As we have seen, the extant volumes of Marx's poetry were written between 1835 and 1837 following the ban on the Young Germans which had condemned those writers as blasphemous and morally seditious. Imitation of the Young Germans for a poet wishing to be published — as Marx did — was thus unwise. Yet, as we have also seen, the apparently safe imitation of Schiller and other poets of the late eighteenth century is symptomatic not so much of a conservative, but of a cautious use of liberal tradition. More than this, both Wyttenbach's use of Schiller's works to illustrate a liberal Kantian philosophy, and Heine's to embody the spirit of liberty suppressed by the censor, point to a reading of Schiller by those known to Marx (either personally or through their writings) which was clearly liberal in a 'modern' sense. Other clues to a 'silent' liberal feeling in Marx's poems, such as his choice of Chamisso as publisher for them in 1837, the choice of personæ such as Prometheus, and the context of radical activity in Trier in which they were written, all add up to a new reading of the young Marx's poetry which refutes the claim that it was only 'Romantic moonshine', or (the claim which even Marx did not make) that it was 'conservative' moonshine.

The years following the ban of 1835 were amongst the most repressive in the history of literary censorship in the Restoration in Germany, and Marx's experience of the period is reflected in his first published articles on censorship and the freedom of the press in 1842. In his poetry, however, this experience has, until this point in our analysis, largely been seen to be reflected 'through a glass darkly', in the 'silences' on the issues censored in 1835. Yet there are amongst the satires and epigrams in the poems also explicit reflections on the subjects which had brought Heine and other Young German poets to the eye of the censor. Some of these epigrams are those on the writer Pustkuchen who, between 1821 and 1828, had published an attack on Goethe which pretended to be the promised sequel to Goethe's novel *Wilhelm Meisters Lehrjahre* (the *Wanderjahre*), and came to be known as the *falsche Wanderjahre*.

The Young Germany had included writers who, while attacking Goethe's lack of political commitment, had defended him against

attacks on the dangerous sensualism of his later works such as the
Römische Elegien, from pietists and other Biedermeier critics.
Pustkuchen had been one of the strongest critics of the sensualistic
Goethe, and had been attacked for it by Heine in his *Romantische
Schule*. Marx again takes up, therefore, a subject which had contributed to the ban on Heine in 1835, and which he knows to be
dangerous. The Pustkuchen epigrams are, moreover, those whose
title is written in, as if it were an after-thought to the Table of
Contents in the volume for the father. Like *Scorpion und Felix*, they
have been a late addition, though (unlike the novel) they can be dated
as having been written earlier than 1837, in 1836.

Marx's first two epigrams on Pustkuchen parodistically imitate
Pustkuchen's demand for Schiller to be more religious and Goethe to
be more moral. Pustkuchen speaks:

> Pustkuchen. (falschen Wanderjahren)
> ### 1.
> Schiller, meint er, sei leidlich gewesen,
> Hätt' er nur mehr in der Bibel gelesen,
>   Seine Glocke sei gar ein trefflich Gedicht
>   Enthielt es nur noch die Auferstehungsgeschicht',
>   Und wie auf einem Eselein,
>   Christus zog in die Stadt hinein,
> Auch sollt' er dem Wallnstein hinzu noch fügen,
> Von Davids Sieg und Philisterzügen.
>
> ### 2.
>   Göthe sei für Frauen ein Grauen,
>   Denn er passe nicht grad' für alte Frauen,
> Er habe ja nur die Natur ergriffen,
> Sie nicht mit Moral zurechtgeschliffen,
>   Hätt' Luthers Katechete sollen studieren,
>   Daraus dann Verse fabriciren.
> Zwar das Schöne hat er manchmal gedacht,
> Doch vergass er zu sagen: 'Gott hab' es gemacht.'

Marx's first epigram refers to Pustkuchen's use of the current debate
over Schiller the poet of moral arguments and Goethe the poet of
aesthetic attitudes. The function of Pustkuchen's half-way defence of
Schiller is to condemn Goethe as immoral, but Marx does not betray
Schiller in defending Goethe against Pustkuchen. Marx defends Goethe

by mocking Pustkuchen and his unwitting distortion of Schiller and of poetry: 'Schiller, he thinks, would have been bearable, If he'd read just a bit more Bible . . .'. In this case Marx's halting rhythms and less than noble phrases parodistically reflect Pustkuchen's lack of talent and wit. The following epigrams, which have Pustkuchen criticising Goethe's lack of morals and dearth of biblical examples, include a parody of Pustkuchen's view of what Faust should have done, and thereby also parody Pustkuchen's attempt to rewrite Goethe in his *Wanderjahre*. Faust, Pustkuchen is made to say, sinned by not paying his debts, and by using his reason: here Marx mocks the morals of Pustkuchen and the Biedermeier philistine, for whom the Bible was important as a puritan ethic, not only for condemning sensualism and sensuousness (and the Young German Saint-Simonians and Goethe), but also for making money. Marx's final epigram in which he plays with a pun on the name of Pustkuchen (which Heine had translated for his French readers as 'omelette soufflé') is also reminiscent of Goethe's own satirical lines on Pustkuchen published in 1836 and entitled *Goethe und Pustkuchen*:

> Will der Pusterich nun gar Pfaffenkuchen pusten,
> Teufelsküchenjungenschar wird den Teig behusten

Marx's concluding epigram reads:

> 'Schlussepigram an den pustenden Meister.'
> So knete deine Kuchen nur zurecht,
> Dann bleibst du immer doch ein Bäckersknecht.
>   Wer wollte auch von dir verlangen,
>   Du solltest dich an Göthen hangen?
> Er hat ja selbst dein Handwerk nicht gekannt,
> Wie käm er zu Genie dann und Verstand?

In his article of November 1847 on Karl Grün's 1846 work, *Über Goethe vom menschlichen Standpunkt*, Engels lists the works in which Goethe attacks authoritarianism in society: *Prometheus, Götz von Berlichingen* and *Faust*. And, although he also accuses Goethe of 'philistinism', Engels calls Grün a philistine for having ignored the 'really great Goethe', the libertine of the *Roman Elegies*. It was of course this Goethe against whom pious citizens such as Pustkuchen had railed. But yet another subject of attack by defenders of Pustkuchen's standpoint in the 1830s was the Saint-Simonian sensualism of the Young Germans. In 1834 Metternich had condemned, in terms similar to those argued earlier by Pustkuchen and in 1835 by Menzel, what he called a new and insidious Goethe cult, comparing it to the morally subversive sensualism of Saint-Simonism then popular in Berlin. Marx's acquaintance (in Berlin in 1837) with one of the members of the salon of Heine's friend and mentor Varnhagen von Ense, Bettina von Arnim, suggests he may have known of the activities of the Berlin Saint-Simonians. He could certainly have also heard Eduard Gans refer to Saint-Simon in his Berlin lectures. But as George Gurvitch has pointed out in his article, 'Saint-Simon et Karl Marx',[1] Saint-Simonism had already been brought to Marx's attention in Trier. Not only could it have been discussed in the Young German Kränzchen, it was present (as mentioned earlier) in the works of the socialist Ludwig Gall, and discussed in the Kasino-Gesellschaft of which both Marx's father and headmaster were members.[2] It has also been generally acknowledged that Marx had heard of Saint-Simon from Jenny von Westphalen's father, while still in Trier.

Marx's attack on Pustkuchen can, in view of Metternich's statement, be seen as belonging to a liberal humanist reaction to the censorship at work in the Restoration. If we follow this lead further, other pieces of historical information and textual evidence appear which point to an attitude in Marx's Romantic and ostensibly apolitical verse, which reflects the rationalism of the Kantian Wyttenbach but also the radicalism of the banned writers of the Young Germany.

In *Scorpion und Felix* of the Addenda to the volume sent to the father in 1837, even more noticeable echoes of the Young German poets are to be found. Whether this is because it was a later edition and not intended for publication, or because prose allowed the pretence at greater objectivity, Marx allows himself more freedom to attack authority and its official mythology in *Scorpion und Felix* than in his poetry, or in the dramatic fragment *Oulanem.* It expresses, moreover, a scepticism about his talent for writing which led Marx in November 1837 to write to his father that he had left his idealistic prose works forever. *Scorpion und Felix* can be dated as one of the last of these poetic works and uses parody not only for purposes of satire, but also to comment on its own epigonal and unsuccessfully imitative nature. Beginning *in media res*, like Sterne's *Tristram Shandy*, it practises literary anarchy self-critically, as a way of reflecting Marx's own failure as a writer. In this atmosphere of *desperance* it plays with erotic and satirical themes similar to those which had led to the banning of the Young Germans and brings to the surface those silences of which symptoms and traces have been found in such works as the epigrams on

Pustkuchen.

Similarly, *Scorpion und Felix* brings to light, by way of explicit reference and literary allusion, those models of the young Marx which clearly belong to the liberal tradition condemned by the Biedermeier, models such as Heine's *Ideen. Das Buch le Grand*, and the 'sensualistic' fragment of a novel of 1836, the memoirs of *Schnabelewopski*. Both Nigel Reeves and S.S. Prawer have traced allusions to these works in Marx's novel. The cook Grethe of *Scorpion und Felix* can, for instance, be seen as a grotesque variation on the cook caricatured by Heine in his *Schnabelewopski*. But she also serves to caricature and 'foreground' other models and literary sources used by the young Marx. Described as a 'bearded beauty' and 'Göttin der Phantasie', but also as the whore of Babylon, Grethe is a caricature of Venus, the 'bearded' star, and goddess of the imagination in Renaissance neo-platonic interpretations of the ancient mythology studied by Marx both as a university student in Bonn and as a schoolboy in the ancient city of Trier. Nicolaevsky points out that a revival of archaeological interest in Trier had occurred at the beginning of the nineteenth century and that classics were avidly studied as part of the town's own history.[3] Marx's own knowledge of the classics bears witness to this, and his parodistic treatment of Greek myth in his youthful novel can be seen as another form of archaeological digging into the past — into, that is, his own past in Trier. This 'archaeology of knowledge' also brings to the surface Goethe and the Young Germans. Thus the bearded Grethe, in representing ugliness which has the teleological function of preventing men from sinning on her account, also parodies Pustkuchen's and other such spiritualists' fear of physical beauty and of sensualism. The bearded Grethe is of course also a parodistic allusion to her namesake Gretchen in Goethe's *Faust*, and it might even be suggested that her name, Grethe, should also be read as an anagram of Goethe. She herself represents the parody resulting from the distortion of Goethe by pietists such as Pustkuchen, but also satirises them by 'unwittingly', in her naïveté, uttering a blasphemous and sensualistic interpretation of John I, on the incarnation of the Word. Grethe's literal understanding of the incarnation of the Word as flesh is erotic and while her blasphemy appears to be spoken from innocence as well as from lack of understanding, it does echo Young Germans such as Heine, Mundt, and Gutzkow, who had also, but intentionally, interpreted the incarnation of the *Logos* literally, as the rehabilitation of the flesh. Thus, while Grethe's blasphemy may be seen as reflecting her lack of religiosity, it also allows Marx to utter blasphemies like those which had brought down the ban of 1835 on the Young Germans.

Quotations such as that from Heine's satire *Frieden* (referred to again by Marx in his letter of November 1837 in which he criticises his poetry as Romantic) also signal a sympathy with the censored Heine which indicates a more 'daring' use of that tradition than is evident in the poetry. The second part of *Frieden*, from which Marx quotes in describing Grethe's eyes as being as 'trivial as the waters of the Spree', had satirised the love of Christian art by the pietist as being based on the love of its market value, and had been omitted from the *Buch der Lieder* when the *Nordsee* cycle in which it had first appeared was reprinted in that book in 1827.

Marx goes on to satirise the romanticism of blue eyes, the utopianism of Mignon, and of the orthodox Goethe. Undergraduate jokes and experiments follow. But amongst them is, in Chapter 22, the return to Ovid's *Tristia*, and, in Chapter 23 (a few lines later), to the figure of Ovid at Tomi, exiled by Augustus because he had more genius (*Genie*) than understanding (*Verstand*). Marx characterises Ovid as the poet of love (for which his works had continued to be banned in Christian Europe before the Renaissance) and though Marx then reduces the scene to one of exaggerated pathos, there is some significance too in his reference to Ovid as the exiled poet, the victim of his monarch, which may relate it to Marx's references to other exiled poets of his own age such as Heine.

As a student reading Law as well as Art History and Classics, Marx was well aware of the relationship of writing to institutions of the state such as the office of the censor. His references to contemporary victims of that institution are rare in his imaginative work, yet a reason for this — the continued practice of that very institution, and the process of self-censorship to which it led — is evidence for, rather than against, Marx's awareness of the existence of both the censor and the liberal writers who were the subject of censorship.

Marx's use of parody in *Scorpion und Felix* (as in the Pustkuchen epigrams) also places the work into the realm of persiflage so disliked by Wolfgang Menzel and condemned by him in the works of Heine and Chamisso. Marx's imitation of the parody of Sterne, E.T.A. Hoffmann and Heine, as well as his parodistic, but sympathetic use of other great writers such as Ovid, Shakespeare and Goethe, can also be seen as part of a dialogue with his past which allows him, at last, to bring models, including those like Heine which had been partly concealed, to the surface for airing and for criticism. But parodistic imitation of these models mixes with the imitation of great parody (such as Sterne's) to confuse the reader sometimes as to the target of Marx's satire. Many books associated with his studies (such as those concerned with Law) are clearly satirised as part of university life from which the young poet wished, temporarily at least, to be liberated: parody, as Kant had also implied, was one means of liberating oneself from past knowledge and this and other functions of Marx's use of parody in *Scorpion und Felix* will be returned to in Part Two of this study. As will be seen there, Marx, while using parody to liberate himself from the books of others, did not find an immediate way of liberating himself from the method of parody after leaving the poetry of his youth in 1837. Like other Young Hegelians he continued to use it as a means of 'smuggling ideas' past the censor, until its own limitations proved to be as restricting as those of censorship itself.

One last reference to the liberating function of parody at the conclusion of *Scorpion und Felix* sums up the 'novel' as a self-conscious exercise in Romantic irony, as well as a self-consciously epigonal / attempt at the genre which, according to another target of Marx's satire, Hegel, had come to its end. Thus Marx caricatures parody's liberating function itself in the story of the emetic given to the dog Bonifacius to free him from his constipation. Even here however a literary model can be found for Marx's parody in the conclusion of Ben Jonson's *Poetaster* and its imitations. Ben Jonson's paradigm of poetic irony, a play satirising the poetaster, ends – as Ian Donaldson writes in *The World Upside Down*[4] – with a parodistic treatment of the theory of catharsis when the character Crispinus is given a 'violent emetic'. As with Marx's novel the final liberation of characters, author, and audience from the bad writer occurs with the conclusion itself. But, unlike Jonson, Marx is being ironic and self-critical, rather than satirical, in doing this.

Yet Marx's imitation of Young German satire and sensualism in *Scorpion und Felix* is an early symptom of the change in his style from an esoteric, ironic mode to a factual and critical one. His thesis of 1841 in which he also quotes Prometheus' words of challenge to the gods (when challenging theology) also explicitly defends epicurean sensualism and Lucretius (banned by the Early Church) against Christian exegesis and allegorisation, or, that is, against the concealment of the sensual in an esoteric or misleading style. At the end of that same year Marx begins the criticism of the new instruction on press freedom which he finishes in February 1842. And Marx's 'sensualistic' passages in the novel of 1837 also represent a heresy in Kantian terms, in the sense that for both Kant and Schiller thought (*cogito*) represented activity, but 'sensuousness' passivity. As sensuousness or *Sinnlichkeit* represented the physical perception of nature, the realm of necessity, it was, like necessity, limited; whereas thought, or cognition, represented freedom from necessity. Wit, as Kant wrote in his *Anthropologie*, was to play a role in this 'liberating' function of thought.

In *Scorpion und Felix*, however, Marx uses wit to liberate himself from the strictures of the censorship of the sensual. Thus it could be said that on the one hand he follows Kant in using wit to liberate himself and his readers from preconceptions, but that, since these preconceptions are in this case the silencing of discussion on sensualism, he is also using wit for a task which contradicts Kant. As Herbert Marcuse argues in *Eros and Civilization*,[5] progress for Kant consisted in the subjugation of the sensuous faculties to reason and the moral sense.[6] The Enlightenment concept of censorship as the 'rational' control of the sensuous and a part of the civilising and enlightening function of the state was based on a similar argument for the repression of the sensuous. Thus, while Marx on the one hand imitates the late eighteenth-century poetry of Schiller, his defence of the sensualism of Goethe against Pustkuchen, and his imitation of the 'licentious' style of the Young Germans in *Scorpion und Felix*, may also be seen as contradicting the Kantian belief in the necessity for the senses to be subjugated to reason. And it was together with this rejection of his 'idealist' poetry that, it will be recalled, Marx also announced the rejection of his old Kantian beliefs in Hegelianism, and, in particular, the Kantian dichotomy between 'what is' and 'what ought to be'. Marx's juvenilia experiment with a range of liberal ideas, and many of these can be categorised as belonging to the late eighteenth-century Kantianism of his father and headmaster. But we have also argued that his defence of sensualism in the epigrams on Pustkuchen and in *Scorpion und Felix* indicates not only a growing oppositional tone to accepted conservative mores in his written work, but also an opposition to the process of repression as such, to censorship as well as to the Enlightenment belief in its ability to 'liberalise' the State through control.[7]

Conclusion

Marx's poetry has suffered from having been categorised — by Marx himself — as 'Romantic moonshine'. For it has subsequently been ignored, avoided, and even 'lost'. And amongst those critics who have taken it up some have defended it as 'realistic', while others have simply equated Romanticism and conservatism and condemned it from this as well as from an aesthetic point of view. Yet Marx's rejection of his poetry as 'romantic' and 'idealistic' in November 1837 can be said to primarily have had the function of freeing him from that part of his past, rather than as having had the purpose of scientifically describing the character of his early imaginative work. In many of the arguments for and against the designation of Marx's youthful poetic works as romantic and conservative, or as idealistic, the context of their composition and the nature of his models have also been disregarded or misunderstood.

A study of the context, and a closer reading of works such as *Scorpion und Felix* and the epigrams on Pustkuchen show, however, that Marx was both aware of the work of his liberal contemporaries, such as the Young German Heine, and of the censorship which prohibited their publication as well as their imitation. With the ban on the Young Germany of 1835 — which was echoed in Trier by the dismissal of Wyttenbach and the arrest of one of his pupils for writing political verse — Marx's more radical models are eliminated. He is left with Schiller, the Romantics and the *Sturm und Drang* poets of the late eighteenth century, given him by Wyttenbach, but also praised by Heine and some other Young Germans for their defence of the freedom taken away by censorship.

Marx's poetic works contain clues to a process of self-censorship symptomatic of a tightening of control and of the external censor condemned by him in his articles of 1842. Thus, while his poems are indeed modelled on idealist and Romantic writers, they do not reflect a conservative mind but an interest in the themes of freedom and harmony shared by the censored poets of the Young Germany. In the many poems dealing with *Zerrissenheit* and with the absence of liberty and harmony Marx touches upon yet another aspect of the elimination of freedom by authoritarian institutions. In analysing these poems Arnold Künzli, like others interested in Marx's psycho-biography, has concentrated on interpreting the demand for liberty and harmony as a reaction of Marx himself against the recipient of the poems of 1837, against his father. While this interpretation bears investigation, it should not exclude consideration of Marx's discussion of other, different or related forms of authoritarian control over the writer, such as that attempted by the pietist critic Pustkuchen and his friend the censor. Though these may be seen as extensions of the authoritarian father, and of his enlightenment philosophy of the rational control of the sensual (as well as the father's opposition to Marx's love for Jenny), they must also, in view of the reasons set out in the preceding pages of this study, be taken seriously as targets of Marx's satire in their own right.

From the point of view of the Enlightenment philosophy which much of Marx's poetry 'versifies', the writing of poetry in itself represents the belief in the importance of an 'aesthetic education', as Schiller was to call his Kantian programme. But it also, as we have seen, represents an attempt at aesthetic expression in the face of increasingly stricter censorship of literature, of, that is, the means to the aesthetic education.

We have also argued that Marx's own condemnation of his poetry as 'Romantic moonshine' led to a new 'censorship' of his works, which was sometimes based on the assumption that they were works of conservative Romanticism. Such a judgement is ironic in view of the fact that it can be shown that the 'Romantic' models imitated by Marx were largely of a late eighteenth-century liberal character, and that they were replacing the contemporary liberal writers banned in 1835. They conceal a 'silence' in Marx's early works on his contemporaries which evidence suggests was a reaction to the censorship of those writers. Marx's awareness of the 'silencing' effect of censorship was only to be made explicit in February 1842, in his article on the new press instruction of December 1841, and even then it had — after a delay of one year — to be 'shouted' out from across the Swiss border from a Swiss publishing house, though later articles on the debates in Parliament had already appeared in the *Rheinische Zeitung*. By this time, however, Marx had liberated himself from the 'idealist' poetry of his youth (if not from the use of parody as a method of criticism), and made no further attempt to explain it. Any edition or interpretation of the poetry must place it into its proper historical context, but this, as the following section will argue, has not always been done.

Notes

1. Georges Gurvitch, 'Saint-Simon et Karl Marx', in *Revue Internationale de Philosophie*, vol. 14, 1969, pp. 399-416.
2. Gurvitch, ibid., points out that the Gesellschaft had been accused of aiding Gall.
3. Nicolaevsky, p. 3.
4. Ian Donaldson, *The World Upside Down*, London, 1970.
5. Herbert Marcuse, *Eros and Civilization*, London, 1956, p. 147.
6. Wilhelm von Humboldt, in his analysis of 'The Limits of State Action' (J.W. Barrow (ed.), Cambridge, 1969), of 1791-2, in which he defended individual freedom in the making of moral decisions, against state intervention, also defended the excitation of sensations by the fine arts, and attempted (p. 74) to

go further than had Kant in his *Critique of Judgement* in defending sensualism. The shyness of the age in arguing such a case is, however, reflected in von Humboldt's conclusion (p. 78): '. . . in these remarks on sensualism I intended to win for it greater freedom and esteem. Still, I must not forget that sensualism is also the source of innumerable physical and moral evils.'

7. Leonard Krieger argues in his *Essays on the Theory of Enlightened Despotism*, Chicago, 1975, that there is an acknowledged contradiction in the eighteenth-century doctrine of government by the rule of reason which argues that reason will serve both to enlarge and to restrict power. As Krieger shows, this contradiction could lead to repression being practised by governments in the name of reason, but the cases of Joseph II and Francis I also show that distinctions between personalities and historical conditions do also affect the way in which the theory of enlightened despotism worked in favour either of liberalism or of authoritarianism.

In his introduction to the first half-volume of volume I/1 of the historical-critical edition of Karl Marx and Friedrich Engels (MEGA),[1] David Riazanov announced the republication of two poems of the young Marx which had appeared under the title *Wilde Lieder* (angry songs) in the fourth number of the Berlin weekly, *Athenäum*, of 23 January 1841.[2] He commented there that it had first become generally known that Marx had written poetry in his youth from the letter to his father of 10 November 1837, published by Marx's daughter, Eleanor, in October 1897. It is this letter which was republished by Riazanov with the newly discovered 1837 collection of poetry in 1929, in the second half-volume of volume I/1. Previously, in his introduction to the first half-volume of 1927, Riazanov could tell us only of Mehring's description of three volumes of poetry written by Marx in October and November 1836 and sent to his betrothed, Jenny von Westphalen, in December 1836, entitled *Buch der Liebe*, volumes I and II, and *Buch der Lieder*. It is these volumes which were 'rediscovered' in 1954 and 1960 by the Moscow Institute.[3] Significantly, the 'lost' poetry was returned to the Institute after the thaw in Soviet censorship following the death of Stalin.

In volume one (of 1975) of the new English edition (published by Lawrence and Wishart) of the *Collected Works* of Marx and Engels several of the poems to Jenny from the lost 1836 volumes have also been translated. In a note to these poems the editors described how two of the lost volumes of 1836 (but with their title-pages missing) had been left to the Institute of Marxism-Leninism of the CC CPSU in 1954 by Marx's grandson, Edgar Longuet, and how, in 1960, the great-grandson, Marcel Charles Longuet, had 'presented the Institute with the third album'. The poems have been reprinted in part in the 'Ergänzungsband, Erster Teil' (Berlin, 1968) of the Marx/Engels *Werke* published by the Institute, and now, in full in the new edition of the MEGA, volume I/1 (Berlin, 1975).

Riazanov mentions seeing the poems of Marx (that is, the three volumes described as containing Romantic verses by Mehring in his

work *Aus dem literatischen Nachlass von Marx und Engels* and rediscovered in 1954 and 1960) in the Lafargue household in 1911, from
where they passed on the death of Lafargue to Jean Longuet. When
asked of their whereabouts by Riazanov in 1925, Longuet claimed to
have lost possession of the manuscripts and was unable to remember
to whom they had been lent, suggesting they may still have been with
Mehring. At that time, when the three volumes mentioned by Mehring
had still not been found, but shortly after the publication of the 1927
volume of the MEGA, inquiries made by the Institute of the
descendants of Marx's friend Dr Roland Daniels of Cologne (who had
been the executor of the library left by Marx in Cologne in 1851) led
to the discovery of the previously unknown collection of songs for
Marx's father of 1837, as well as a book of folk-lore songs which Marx
had collected from other folk-song collections for Jenny in 1839,
when he had apparently stopped writing poetry himself. Mehring, who
begins his chapter on the poems with the statement that he is doubtful
as to 'whether he should discuss them',[4] writes that Madame Laura
Lafargue had handed him the now lost volumes of Marx's verse saying
that 'her father had treated the verses with very little respect, and that
her parents had laughed about the follies of youth whenever they
spoke of the poems'.

In the early 1900s Mehring had laid a foundation for the 'appropria-
tion of the classical heritage of German literature' (of Herder, Goethe,
Schiller and others) to the working class of Germany (which was later
taken up in the German Democratic Republic), by writing many
introductions on the writers of the classical tradition, as well as on
those ignored or damned by the bourgeoisie, such as the Young
Germans. Mehring's attitude to Chamisso as a defender of the principle
of liberty[5] is not unlike Heine's and, as we have argued, Marx's. His
comments on Schiller's liberal humanism were more ambivalent than
Heine's (being written under historical circumstances different from
those which determined Heine's praise of Schiller, under the censorship
of direct discussion of the nineteenth-century Revolutions), so that
while he condemned the Idealism of Schiller, celebrated by the bourgeoisie, he also described the victory of the proletariat as realising
Schiller's aesthetic aims by harmonising the ideal with reality.[6] Ironically, it could also be said that Mehring's earlier condemnation of Marx's
Romantic verses as trivial was also made from within a Kantian
aesthetic. Yet another irony, though of a more serious nature, was that
Mehring himself was subjected to criticism in the 1930s by Lukács and
others for adhering to the Kantian tradition without giving due regard

to the more official theories of Realism, such as that of art as
Widerspiegelung.[7]

It was in the face of criticism of Marx's poems as 'Romantic follies',
and the suggestion that they should perhaps not be published as part of
his *oeuvre*, that Riazanov searched for the lost volumes in 1927 and
published the newly found collection of verses of 1837 in 1929. The
policy of the MEGA to publish all of Marx's works meant that the
juvenilia too were to be printed. Yet in 1929 Riazanov does not only
have to justify the publication of Romantic works in Marx's *oeuvre*
against the criticisms of Mehring and others, but, having been an
observer at the 15th Party Congress of 1927 in which Stalin defeated
the policies of Trotsky, Zinoviev and Kamenev, he is also aware of the
plans for industrialisation and collectivisation which included the
subjugation of literature to a tool of the state. Riazanov did not live to
see the formation of the Soviet Writers' Union and Zhdanov's pro-
clamation of the theory of Socialist Realism in 1934, having died in
one of Stalin's camps in the early 1930s. But his awareness of the need
to place Marx's poetic attempts into the context of Realism in publishing them as foot-notes to Marx's *oeuvre*[8] is evident in his Introduction
of 1929. Though Riazanov himself appears to be clear about the fact
that Marx's realism was based on Idealist presuppositions, some other
analyses of Marx's poetic works have appeared which assume that the
apparent realism of Marx's satire represents a rejection of Idealism as
early as 1836 and 1837 in his work.

Though Riazanov agrees with Mehring that many of the poems are
of little talent and of a Romantic character, he then argues that some of
the poems in the newly discovered collection of 1837 exhibit a
realistic approach in dealing with material based on the Berlin which
Marx experienced as a student in 1836 and 1837. Yet he also makes it
clear that Marx was attacking the 'prosaic realism of the philistine' in
these satires, from the point of view of a Kantian ethic and aesthetic.
Riazanov wrote of the realistic background to these attacks on philistine realism:

Das literarische und kulturelle Leben des damaligen Berlin, aktuelle
wissenschaftliche und philosophische Kämpfe spiegeln sich in ihnen
wider, und ein sehr bestimmtes Urteil des jungen Autors kommt
hier zum Ausdruck[9]

Ironically, Riazanov's use of Marx's satiric epigrams to prove Marx
a realist — if only within the limits of Kantian Idealism — might not

even have been acceptable to Zhdanov, for whom satire was a negative form of literature, in contrast to Socialist Realism, which was a style which said 'yes' to life.[10] Even now the study of parody — traditionally the language of the underground — which was newly developed by Russian Formalists such as Tynjanov, Shlonsky, and Bachtin in the 1920s, is not often discussed in Soviet criticism, though it must also be added that, for various reasons, it has often been ignored by others. In eighteenth-century Vienna, where the censor Sonnenfels had banned the *Hanswurst*, and in Germany, where Gottsched had given satire a bad name in criticism, parody and irony (even as used in Cervantes' *Don Quixote*) were generally considered to be techniques suited to the broadsheet but not to serious literature. The Formalists of the twentieth century argued, however, that as a meta-fictional form of literary criticism, parody could tell us more not only about the processes of writing than other literary forms, but also about the relationship of literature to life, and of authority to both literature and life. Bachtin's extension of this in his analysis of Rabelais, to an exploration of the links between parody and the carnival as two archetypal forms of using laughter to liberate the subjects of authority from that authority, was particularly challenging.

It was, in fact, as Riazanov realised, exactly in those satires in which glimpses of Marx's student-life and lectures are to be had, that Marx condemned Realism and Materialism as aesthetic and philosophical standpoints. Although Marx's recourse to satire in order to attack these views may appear to represent a turning away from lyric Romanticism, satire was for Schiller, in its mockery of reality which did not match up to the ideal, symptomatic of the loss of harmony with nature of the *sentimentalischer Dichter*, later identified with by the Romantics. Schiller's concept of satire is also based on a Kantian dualism soon to be rejected by Marx. In form alone then, the satires are not works of nineteenth-century Realism. Marx's own evaluation of the poetry, which he makes in the letter to his father of 10 November 1837, as idealistic, and as presenting a false picture of reality, may be a more honest one than those which attempt to justify the satires as realistic and overlook their idealism. The confessional letter also tells us that Marx had written other unpublished poems and short stories which he had burnt after an illness and his conversion to Hegel's philosophy, at the time of his entrance into the *Doktorklub* (in autumn 1837), where he had met Bauer, Ruge, and other Young Hegelians. In his letter of 10 November Marx uses the same Hegelian language to describe his Romantic poetry and his allegiance to the philosophy of Kant and

Fichte when writing his *Philosophie des Rechts*, as being fallaciously based on the distinction between that which is and that which should be.[11] One work which Marx's father refers to in discussing one of Marx's 'more obscure' poems (MEGA I (2), 187) was Kant's *Anthropologie*, referred to earlier. In this work we also find clues to an idealist's aesthetic of satire which helps to put Marx's sense of satire into a wider context, and, specifically, into the context of Enlightenment thought outlined in the early discussion of censorship. For Kant, man, the subject of the *Anthropologie*, had been best represented in literature in the realistic if exaggerated characterisation of types by authors such as Richardson and Molière. Kant had then gone on to praise the wit of the parodist Fielding as acting as a further corrective to the preconceptions of man given in novels such as Richardson's *Clarissa*. Kant, the idealist, praises both realism and satire in such passages, and it is clear that he saw nothing incompatible between his philosophy and literary realism and satire. For Schiller too, as has been said, satire could serve the idealist by comparing reality to the ideal. It was only after his break with Kantianism, and after leaving the writing of poetry, that Marx rejected Kant's distinction between 'what is' and 'what ought to be', and, as he wrote to his father on 10 November 1837,[12] 'arrived at the point of seeking the idea in reality itself', and at Hegel.

The problem of reading Marx's epigrams on Hegel as a defence of Hegel's Realism will be discussed in a following section. It is clear that although Marx's 'realistic satires' may be called Romantic or idealist they do not necessarily defend conservative or orthodox ideals. Riazanov also acknowledges this in his Introduction (MEGA I/1 (2), XIV) when he singles out the epigrams on Pustkuchen as a 'protest against conservatism'.

One other mystery surrounding the collection of poems written by Marx for his father in 1837 as published by Riazanov in 1929 was the disparity between the Table of Contents said to have been written by Marx, and the contents of the collection as it appeared. Riazanov did not, moreover, make it clear if the collection of poems found in the possession of Dr Daniels was the edition sent by Marx to his father or a copy kept by Marx. Although the existence of poems not explicitly listed in Marx's Table of Contents and the fact that it has been shown[13] that Marx added some works later, may imply that the latter is possible, we cannot be certain. The poems which do not appear in the Table of Contents made by Marx are by and large the satires. In fact, of the thirteen or so satires in the collection only four groups are listed by

Marx. These are the *Epigramme auf Hegel*, the *Epigramme auf die Deutschen und Pustkuchen*, *Weltgericht*, and *Epigramme und Xenien*. The exact nature of the latter is difficult to judge from their vague title, but it is not altogether clear that all of the other nine satires would have been grouped together under this title, for some of them are not typical epigrams or *Xenien*. The satires not listed appear in the collection edited by Riazanov in alternation with the ballads and romances. The effect of this on the reader tends to be that the Romantic poems are continuously put into a more 'realistic' light. Occasionally (as in the case of the *Wiener Affentheater in Berlin* which follows *Die Zauberharfe*), the appearance of a satire after a romance will even create the impression that it has the function of parodying the Romantic ideals of the verses which precede it.

Knowing that Riazanov is conscious of having to defend his decision to publish Romantic poems similar to those criticised by Mehring as unworthy of Marx's name, one was tempted to ask if the alternation of romances and satires was an editorial construct rather than a reflection of Marx's plan of 1837. Certainly the combination of romances and satires appears to reflect no inner logic suggested otherwise in the collection. The recent edition of the poetry suggests, however, that this had resulted from Marx's addition of satires to the romances at a later date, when he wrote them into the unwritten sides of the pages bearing the romances. While this was no doubt necessitated by the lack of space left after the romances in the book, Marx's growing scepticism about his Romantic verse might also be taken into account in asking why he allowed the resulting mixture of romances (that is, love poems and hymns) and satires to take shape as it did.

Riazanov must be acknowledged as a sensitive as well as a competent editor of Marx's poetry. But it must also be said that he has been speculative in stating (perhaps as further justification for the publication of the Romantic works) that the 1837 volume containing this mixture of romances and more 'realistic' satires had shown an improvement on the others of a few months earlier, which, according to Mehring, contained 'with only one exception' love lyrics and fantastic romances and ballads.[14] Riazanov had not had the possibility of comparing the two collections closely and it would even appear from the New MEGA that some of the satires of 1837 had already been written down in 1836. All four volumes never appear to have been examined closely by one of the concerned critics — Mehring ironically having seen the three volumes of 1836, which were then lost, but not the 1837 collection for Marx's father discovered after 1927. As none of Marx's collections of poetry had benefited from an objective editor at that time it was thus speculative for Riazanov to suggest that poems of the 1837 volume were amongst the best of those books.

The volumes of poetry published in the new MEGA I/1 span the years 1833 to 1837. They are:

> *Buch der Liebe. I. Teil* (Autumn 1836)
> *Buch der Liebe. 2. Teil* (November 1836)
> *Buch der Lieder* (November-December 1836)
> *Gedichte, meinem teuren Vater zu seinem Geburtstage 1837* (1837)
> *Gedichte aus den Jahren 1835 und 1836. Zusammengestellt von Sophie Marx* (1835-6)
> *Gedichte. Aus einem Notizbuch von Sophie Marx* (1833-7)

Some poems appear more than once in the collection.[15] There is also a collection of *Volkslieder*, gathered from various sources by Marx for Jenny in 1839.

The volume for the father's birthday in April 1837 (of 177 manuscript pages), which Riazanov published in 1929, has been re-edited and reprinted with some alterations. Contradictions, or alternatives, to Riazanov's edition are not always made explicit. It would appear, however, that Riazanov had printed the poems consecutively, as they appeared in the hand-written manuscript,[16] while the editors of the new MEGA have printed them as they see Marx having written them. They argue that differences in ink and handwriting demonstrate that Marx had written those on the left-hand side of the *Inhaltsverzeichnis* (the Table of Contents) first, and then added those on the right-hand side in the spare pages left to him afterwards. The editors do not suggest how long after the first group of poems the second group was added. If all were sent to the father in 1837 the difference in time could not have been that great and Marx's additions to the volume would then seem rather to indicate the absence of any significant plan.

One question not raised by the editors, however, is whether Marx added epigrams such as those on Pustkuchen (the title of which is squeezed into the Table of Contents as an afterthought) after giving the manuscript to his father. The epigrams, as stated earlier, had been written as early as 1836, but it is not impossible that, despite their defence of Goethe, Marx may have considered leaving them out of the volume for his father in view of their irreverent comments on religion and society. Such speculations raise other questions however, such as that of the father's attitude to satirical comments on his milieu. Though a reader of Kant's *Anthropologie* and involved with Wyttenbach in the Kasino-Gesellschaft banquet, Marx's father also plays the role of the upright Prussian civil servant when writing to his son.

The manuscript of 1837 used by the editors of the new MEGA is that found by Riazanov, and taken from the library of Dr Daniels. As it was with Dr Daniels in Cologne that Marx left his books in 1851 before leaving for London, it is most likely that he had received the volume back from his father (or possibly after the latter's death in 1838) and had been able to add works to it then — if not before. Though they are added to the equally satiric Hegel epigrams, the satires criticising the pious Pustkuchen were a more daring offering to the father than the defence of Kant and Fichte contained in the Hegel epigrams and Marx could well have hesitated about adding them. This consideration might be applied as well to what the editors call the 'more realistic' epigrams and Xenien (also added later) which deal with Berlin. It may also be doubted that Marx added these 'realistic' epigrams for his father because, as the editors claim,[17] he thought so much of them, if it can be argued that he may originally have left them out for reasons such as those just suggested. This type of argumentation is, of course, highly speculative, but if Marx did add the more satiric epigrams after sending the volume to the father and after deciding not to publish, they might also be seen as redressing the balance between satire and romance upset by the self-censorship which can be seen in Marx's choice of older models and which was a common reaction of writers to the 1835 ban on the Young Germans.

But it must again be emphasised that many of these epigrams described by both Riazanov and the editors of the poetry in the new MEGA, are not in a materialist's, but in an idealist's sense 'realistic'. As stated briefly earlier, satire was for Schiller, for example, one of the literary forms available to the 'sentimental' poet to attack the discrepancy between reality and the ideal, and Marx uses it in this manner as we have seen in his epigrams. His satires on the *Mediziner* are, for example, realistic in the sense that they deal with university life experienced by Marx in Berlin, but these satires (which attack the reduction of anthropology to physical and biological factors) also offer an attack on the crude realism of positivistic science. In lines attacking mathematicians Marx even echoes the Romantic Novalis' famous lines criticising the antipathy of Newtonian science to the imagination, which begin:

Wenn nicht mehr Zahlen und Figuren (When numbers and figures,)
Sind Schlüssel aller Kreaturen . . . (No longer give us the key to all
     creatures)

Marx's epigrams also attack the superficiality of scientific explanations:

. . . Mit Streichen die Welt gemessen,
Haben nie den Geist herausgefressen.

(. . . Having measured the world with pen strokes,
They still cannot find its real ghost.)[18]

The young Marx's use of satire is almost without exception directed
towards the defence of Kantian Idealism and the poetry of Schiller,
the Romantics, and of Goethe against philistinism and materialism.
Later, in *The German Ideology*, as Robert Tucker points out,[19] positive
science was for Marx to take over from where speculation ended in real
life. There might even be said to be a form of break between Marx's
creative writing of 1837 and his conversion to Hegelianism. But this first
'break' in Marx's thought, from Kantian dualism to Hegelian philosophy may be characterised by a change to an alternative school of
thought, rather than by the discovery of a new method or a new subject-
matter. In this sense the conversion to Hegel in 1837, which Marx
describes at the time as a 'turning-point' in his life, cannot be called an
'epistemological' break. One of the contradictions which it appears to
leave Marx with, and which becomes one of the factors contributing
to the crisis which precedes the break in 1845, is that Marx continues
to use the methods of criticism and the satire he had previously. This is
another of the central problems in this study: the nature of the continuity in Marx's and Engels' use of satire and parody from their
juvenilia, through their Young Hegelian works, to *The German Ideology*
and following writings.
     The satires entitled *An die Mediziner* provide clear evidence that in
1837 the young Marx was antipathetic towards the positive sciences;
they condemn, for instance, medical scientists as philistines:

Verdammt Philistermedizinerpack,
Die ganze Welt ist euch ein Knochensack . . .[20]

(Damned philistine pack of medicos,
The world is for you just a sack of bones . . .)

These scientists are also attacked for thinking it is in their power to give life as well as to heal it, and for seeing the Creator from an inverted perspective, as being intelligent because he must have known so much anatomy:

> Der Herrgott sei ein Witzkopf gewesen,
> Dass er so sehr in der Anatomie belesen.
>
> (The Lord God must have been a whizz-kid
> To know all the anatomy that he did.)

Their 'materialism' is seen to conflict with any argument for the existence of God. Marx derives humour from the application of their perspective to theology and, while he may appear to defend the latter, he also satirises it too in the course of caricaturing science. Marx's attack in these satires on prosaic materialism is consistent with the argument in the opening poem to the volume of 1837, *Schöpfung*, that creation and creating is something divine. His method of satire — of comparing the ideal to reality to prove the latter in conflict with the former — is again similar to that described by Schiller in his essay *Über naïve und sentimentalische Dichtung*. Again the satires tend to support rather than undermine the idealist nature of the other poems. The argument for creation as a divine activity is, moreover, that of the *Sturm und Drang* poets of the 1770s, for whom the highest ideal of the poet was that of the 'Genie', the creative genius. Like Faustus and Prometheus, the Genie was in perpetual activity. The *Sturm und Drang* was in fact also known as the *Geniezeit*. Although the Young German poets of the 1830s also described themselves as a second *Sturm und Drang* they had eschewed the *Kunstperiode* concept of genius and Marx's defence of the idea of genius is closer to that given by Kant in his *Anthropologie* than to that of his contemporaries. Only in *Scorpion und Felix* does Marx appear to express the Young German's more sceptical view of genius, and share their concept of the writer as epigonal.

   The following *Mediziner* satires attack the teleological view of nature as a source of herbal cures, and the attribution of psychological states to physical causes:

> Wer des Abends Nudeln und Klösse verschluckt,
> Der wird des Nachts — von Träumen gedruckt.

(He who eats noodles and dumplings at evening
Will be oppressed at night by his dreaming.)

Marx is at this point very far from materialism: he caricatures their
brand of anthropomorphism as distorting the psychology of man.
So, in *Mediziner-Metaphysik*, the scientists' search for the soul in the
stomach is satirised as an inappropriate method of verification for
an ontological argument, and their failure to find the soul is rejected
as proof for its non-existence: again the discrepancy between Idealism
and Realism in the satires is used to attack the latter rather than the
former. As Marx's letter of 10 November 1837 argues, his poems begin
from the assumption that the ideal is the measure for the real.

As we shall later argue, one of the problems in interpreting the
Hegel-Epigramme as an attack on Kantian Idealism, as some critics
have done, is that they must then contradict this standpoint given in
the *Mediziner* satires of the same collection. It has been argued[21] that
Marx's aversion to pure materialism – to materialism which had no real
explanation for consciousness – remained with him through the
critique of materialism in the *Holy Family* of 1844 to his development
of the theory of historical materialism. But it is important to specify
that the *Mediziner* satires attack materialism from what is clearly an
idealist standpoint – and one which sees Idealism parodied in the
materialist's supposition that matter and not mind gives order to the
world. Marx mocks the materialist scientists for this by showing that a
materialist explanation of mind is absurd. Their world is, for the
idealist, *verkehrt*, or upside down. When the world is turned the right
way up again by the idealist's satire, the idealist explanation of matter
as subject to the order given it by the mind will be proven right: and
the world of the *Mediziner* will be shown to be out of joint, because
they have reduced the mind to a category of matter.

Although the satires are written with little of the bombast of the
ballads and romances, they also – when compared with models such as
Heine's anti-philistine satire in Part II of the poem *Frieden* of the
Nordsee, from which Marx quotes in his letter of 10 November 1837
(and again in *Scorpion und Felix*) – appear less artful than those of his
contemporaries. They have the character of undergraduate humour and
make less use of paradox and irony than the traditional epigram, as can
be seen from a comparison with Lichtenberg's or with the *Xenien* of
Schiller and Goethe. These consist of two-lined distichons, which assist
in making the satiric use of paradox in the epigram pointed. This is the
form disliked by Menzel in the work of Heine and Chamisso and despite

the obvious contrast in talent, Marx's epigrams are close in style and technique to Heine's anti-philistine satires.[22] But like Goethe's and Schiller's *Xenien* they also echo the Latin epigrams, popular in the Renaissance, which were perhaps known to Marx from a reading of Martial and Propertius.[23] The following analysis of Marx's *Hegel-Epigramme* attempts to clarify some of the problems which have led to numerous misinterpretations of those works by both literary critics and Marxologists. In order not to over-emphasise the aesthetic value of the satires they are treated here as an appendix to this section on the discussion of the Romantic v. Realistic character of Marx's poetry.

Notes

1.   Published for the Marx-Engels-Institute Moscow, in Frankfurt-am-Main, in 1927.

2.   MEGA I/1 (i), XXXVI. It was these two works which led Mehring to think, wrongly, that Marx had continued writing Romantic verse up until 1841.

3.   See New MEGA I/1, Berlin, 1975. Michail Lifshitz does not appear to know of the return of the manuscripts in 1959 when he completes his study of 'Marx and Aesthetics' in Moscow. (See *Karl Marx und die Ästhetik*, Dresden, 1960, p. 41.)

4.   F. Mehring, *Aus dem literarischen Nachlass von Marx und Engels*, 3rd edn., Stuttgart, 1920, vol. 1, p. 25.

5.   See Mehring's *Zur deutschen Literatur von 1830-1848* (1910).

6.   See 'Vorwort zur 2. Auflage' of *Schiller − Ein Lebensbild für deutsche Arbeiter* (1909).

7.   The theory of art as *Widerspiegelung* will be discussed in a later section. It involves discussing art as the reflection of the social conditions which are at its base.

8.   Marx's poetic works are described in Riazanov's Introduction of 1929 to the MEGA I/1 (2) as part of the *Ergänzungen* and *Nachträge* to the works published in the first half-volume.

9.   MEGA I/1 (2), XIII.

10.   Harold Swayze, *Political Control of Literature in the USSR, 1946-1959*, Cambridge, Mass., 1962, p. 39.

11.   MEGA I/1 (2), p. 215.

12.   Marx's letter to his father of 10 November 1837 is translated in full in *Karl Marx. Friedrich Engels. Collected Works*, vol. 1, Lawrence and Wishart, London, 1975, pp. 10-21.

13.   New MEGA I/1, Berlin, 1975, Apparat.

14.   Franz Mehring, *Karl Marx − The Story of His Life*.

15.   See Apparat to New MEGA I/1 (1975), p. 1220 ff.

16.   Now held in the Karl Marx Haus, Trier.

17.   New MEGA 1975, Apparat I/1, p. 1238.

18.   *Geist* is spirit. *Streichen* is either strokes or strides, and Marx uses the ambiguity ironically.

19.   Robert Tucker, *Philosophy and Myth in Karl Marx*, 2nd edn., Cambridge, 1972, p. 179 ff.

20.   MEGA I/1 (2), p. 16.

21.   See Sidney Hook, *From Hegel to Marx*, p. 274.

22.   In the letter to Marx of 12 April 1841 Bruno Bauer had referred to a poem by Heine as an *Epigramm*. MEGA I/1 (2), p. 252.

23.   Ibid., p. 194. Marx heard A.W. Schlegel lecture on Propertius' elegies in the summer semester of 1836 in Bonn.

3.2 ANALYSIS: MARX'S *HEGEL. EPIGRAMME*
A Defence of Realism?

HEGEL. EPIGRAMME

1. Weil ich das Höchste entdeckt und die Tiefe sinnend gefunden,
   Bin ich grob, wie ein Gott, hüll' mich im Dunkel, wie er.
   Lange forscht' ich und trieb auf dem wogenden Meer der Gedanken,
   Und da fand ich das Wort, halt' am Gefundenen fest.

   (Because I've revealed the highest and intuited the depths,
   I am brutal, like a god, I cover myself in the dark, like he.
   For a long time I've searched and looked on the undulating sea of
        thoughts,
   And there I found the Word, and hold to this discovery fast.)

2. Worte lehr' ich, gemischt in dämonisch verwirrt Getriebe,
   Jeder denke sich dann, was ihm zu denken beliebt.
   Wenigstens ist er nimmer geengt durch fesselnde Schranken,
   Denn wie aus brausender Flut, stürzend vom ragenden Fels,
   Sich der Dichter ersinnt der Geliebten Wort und Gedanken,
   Und was er sinnet, erkennt, und was er fühlet, ersinnt,
   Kann ein jeder sich saugen der Weisheit labenden Nektar,
   Alles sag' ich euch ja, weil ich ein Nichts euch gesagt!

   (Words I teach, mixed in a daemonically confused machinery,
   So that each can think, what he likes.
   At least he is never restricted by chaining confines,
   For, as the poet from a roaring flood, toppling from the soaring rock,
   Envisages the words and thoughts of the beloved,
   And what he dreams recognises, and what he feels envisages,
   So can each one suck the refreshing nectar of wisdom,
   I tell you everything, in telling you a 'Nothing'!)

3. Kant und Fichte gern zum Äther schweifen,
   Suchten dort ein fernes Land,
   Doch ich such' nur tüchtig zu begreifen,
   Was ich — auf der Strasse fand!

(Kant and Fichte love to soar up into the air,
To search there for a distant country,
But I only try to understand,
What I've found — on the street.)

4. Verzeiht uns Epigrammendingen,
Wenn wir fatale Weisen singen,
Wir haben uns nach Hegel einstudiert,
Auf sein' Ästhetik noch nicht (abgeführt).

(Forgive us epigram-things,
If we sing disagreeable tunes,
We have modelled ourselves on Hegel,
And haven't yet purged (out/onto) his aesthetic.)

Riazanov recognised that many of Marx's attacks on the philistines of his time required contrasting their reality to the ideals of greater men, and here Riazanov admitted to the 'ethical idealism' of some of Marx's satires. Riazanov also acknowledged the critical nature of the epigrams on Hegel which Marx originally entered into the volume in the midst of his romances, while many other Marxologists have misread them as either a defence of Hegel or as a criticism of Kantian Idealism, or both. Yet the persona of Hegel which speaks in the epigrams is clearly also the target of Marx's satire, and a means to a defence of Hegel's targets, Kant and Fichte. Only after sending the poems to his father in 1837 did Marx become 'converted' to the Hegelianism of Berlin, and while Riazanov clearly places the poetry before this 'break' (he uses the word *Umbruch*) in Marx's thought, many others have misunderstood the place of poems like the Hegel epigrams in Marx's biography and epistemography, and read them in the light of what were in fact later philosophical developments in Marx's thought.

At least two critics writing specifically on the poetry have interpreted the *Epigramme* as signs of Marx's conversion — supposedly in the midst of composing the collection — to the more realistic standpoint of Hegelianism.[1] One critic, Nigel Reeves, writing in a journal of German literary criticism, *Oxford German Studies*, maintains that the third epigram — describing Kant and Fichte enthusiastically soaring away from the earth into the 'ether' on their explorations, and the persona as being satisfied with trying to understand what he finds on the street — expresses a 'respect for the empirical that was later to be a central feature of his work',[2] and adds, by way of explanation for this interpretation, that Marx speaks here in the person of Hegel. Reeves makes no attempt to reconcile this alleged swing to empiricism with Marx's attacks on positivism in the satires attacking medical scientists which he has just discussed and he provides, moreover, no textual analysis or supportive evidence to justify his interpretation, which must appear contradictory in the light of both Marx's letter (which he alludes to later)[3] and the tendency of the other poems. Marx does 'speak in the voice of Hegel' in his epigrams, but uses this persona ironically, as a target.

William M. Johnston's article, 'Karl Marx's verse of 1836-1837 as a foreshadowing of his early philosophy'[4] also sees the epigrams as satires written against Kant and Fichte. Yet the confusion lying at the basis of Reeves's argument, that Marx was to be identified with the persona Hegel's attack on Kant and Fichte, is simple compared to the contradictions in the interpretation offered by Johnston. Johnston's fallacy is based in his equation not of Marx and Hegel, but of Hegel with Kant and Fichte as the targets of satire: 'First, he [Marx] embarks upon a satire of Hegel's predecessors in a series of "Epigramme".'[5] This false premise leads Johnston into difficulties of logical interpretation as he continues:

> Although Marx never goes so far as to accuse Hegel of ignoring altogether what he 'finds in the street', he does, as we shall see, judge him to be no less fond than his predecessors of the 'ether' and 'the distant land'. For in another 'Xenion', Marx satirizes the influence of Hegel's abstractions on poets who aspire to apply his 'Ästhetik' in their writing of verse. They are doomed to fail as poets and must apologize for their failure . . .[6]

Johnston then quotes the fourth and final epigram, translating it as:

> Pardon us creatures of epigram   /
> If we sing disagreeable tunes;
> We have schooled ourselves in Hegel
> And from his aesthetic we have not yet been purged.[7]

Having made no distinction between the voices of Marx the author and the persona of Hegel in the preceding epigrams, Johnston is now unable to recognise or acknowledge the sudden use by the author of a different voice, of the epigrams themselves making an ironic apology to the reader for Hegel. In this last epigram Marx speaks of

/ 'we epigram-things' ('uns Epigrammendingen'), which could be taken
to mean just the preceding epigrams, or the epigrams and their
'authors', the persona Hegel (who needs to be apologised for) and the
ironist Marx. The irony of the apology is made clear when, firstly, it is
made in the form of an epigram and, secondly, the point of the epigram introduces an ironically 'realistic' and crudely ambiguous remark
on the influence of Hegel's aesthetic of the author's verse. By these
means the apology is turned into yet another ironic attack on the
persona Hegel.

Johnston's use of Marx's 1844 criticism of 'abstractness' in Hegel,[8]
as a final piece of evidence for his interpretation is both ahistorical
and based on an originally false interpretation of the 1837 text.
Johnston must also gloss over the contradiction between interpreting
the epigrams as criticism of Idealism and interpreting the *Mediziner*
satires as an attack on materialism.[9] The latter show that in 1837 Marx
had not only not reached a position (as perhaps Feuerbach may have)[10]
of attacking Hegel as not being pragmatic enough, but had not even
been converted to the Hegelianism of Bauer. Later, in his dissertation
of 1841, Marx, as Kamenka writes in the *Ethical Foundations of
Marxism*,[11] chose Hegel's monistic Idealism to overcome Kantian
dualism and to 'reconcile that which is and that which ought to be in
the Rational'. In taking up this subject again in the article 'Marxism
and Ethics − A Reconsideration',[12] Kamenka writes that the
problem of resolving the Kantian dualism of 'ought' and 'is' remained,
however, unresolved for Marx. After rejecting the dualism of 'ought'
and 'is' Marx was faced with the problem that rationality 'ought' to
'be':

> For all his suppression of the dualism of 'ought' and 'is' historical
> 'progress' remained for him a normative conception, 'rationality'
> something which one *ought* to support.

Marx's epigrams on Hegel satirise not only Hegel's attack on
Kantian dualism, but the obscurity of the language in which these
criticisms were made. In the first Hegel epigram the 'I' persona of the
poem describes himself as having exhausted the heights and the depths
of an undulating sea of thoughts until, finding 'the Word' − the *Logos*
− he held fast. This 'Word' is described as a rock of certainty in a sea
of uncertainties. The title of the epigrams, though ambiguous, appears
to suggest that the speaker is Hegel, and in the following epigrams the
identity of his Word as the negation of the negation (the *Nichts* in

the dialectic) is made clear. Ironically, certainty is thereby defined as 'nothingness', and the real meaning of the 'Word' is at this point in the epigrams, like Hegel himself, swathed in darkness:

> I am brutal, like a god, I cover myself in the dark, like he.

Hegel, hidden in the darkness, is characterised as a *Dunkelmann*, an obscurantist rather than the *illuminati* or rationalist he was supposed to be. The 'Word' which he finds and holds fast to in this darkness recalls the Logos of the first Chapter of John's Gospel and the concept of theodicy which lay behind Hegel's history of the incarnation of Reason. Yet, unlike Christ as the incarnation of the Word which shines in the darkness, Hegel's word remains obscure. John 1 was one of Marx's favourite biblical passages, as his numerous quotations of it, from *Scorpion und Felix* of 1837 to *The Holy Family* and *The German Ideology* show. The biblical reference is suggested to the reader here by both the positioning of the 'Lord' in 'the darkness', and the description of Hegel as a type of god. As the epigrams progress it becomes clear that while the speaker is to be identified with Hegel he is also the target of Marx's satire. The full stop after the name of Hegel in the title, before the word *Epigramme*, underlies the ambiguity of Hegel's role in the satires as both the target and the persona, the epigram-poet. (Hegel had also written epigrams.)

Marx's satire against Hegel, though sometimes verbally clumsy, does appear to work on several levels at once as well as with ambiguity: as when, for example, the epigrams reduce Hegel's philosophy to nonsense in three stages, ironically reflecting the triadic development of Hegel's dialectic. So, for example, in the second epigram, the philosopher's great discovery, 'the Word', which has served him as a refuge in the undulating sea of thoughts, is changed into its opposite, the target onto which he will be pinned down by the satirist:

> Words I teach, mixed in a daemonically confused machinery,
> So that each can think, what he likes.

For the 'Word' of Epigram 1 is now used in the plural, in its specific (non-symbolic, non-universal) sense in standard language to designate the verbiage listened to by the undergraduate student of Professor Hegel or of his apologists (Hegel's lectures on the philosophy of history had been newly published by Gans in 1837). Now the satirist directs the persona to speak ambiguously of his words (rather than *the* word) as those taught by him but also as those used by him to teach. These are, moreover, described as being mixed up together in a 'daemonically confused' machinery or web, while it is also said that the 'limits' to meaning are missing.

The conclusion that each listener is thus able to think about what he pleases on hearing Hegel, or to interpret the master's words as arbitrarily as he wishes is a travesty, however, of the Hegelian goal of freedom achieved in the Hegelian dialectic when the conscious self transcends its own 'limits'. Robert Tucker writes of the dialectic: 'Spirit's self-realization through cognitive activity is for Hegel a process of the successive transcending of limits'.[13] In the epigrams this freedom is caricatured as a result of confusion rather than of increased knowledge and is also ironically mirrored in the speaker's ambiguous use of words. Ironically then Hegel is condemned by the confused ambiguity of his words, showing freedom through confusion in a further negative light: to Marx's reader the persona's claim to give freedom to his listeners is equally effective as condemnation by the lecturer of his own lack of clarity.

In his letter to his father of 10 November, Marx had gone on to describe his conversion to Hegel as a conversion to his worst enemy. He had, moreover, described the antipathy he had felt towards the Hegelian philosophy as a grotesquely 'rocky melody':

> Ich hatte Fragmente der Hegelschen Philosophie gelesen, deren groteske Felsenmelodie mir nicht behagte. Noch einmal wollte ich hinabtauchen in das Meer, aber mit der bestimmten Absicht, die geistige Natur ebenso notwendig, konkret und festgerundet zu finden wie die körperliche, nicht mehr Fechterkünste zu üben sondern die reine Perle ans Sonnenlicht zu halten.[14]

> (I had read fragments of Hegelian philosophy, the grotesque rocky melody of which had not suited me. I wanted once more, however, to dive into the sea, but with the specific intention to find spiritual nature just as necessary, concrete and well-rounded as material nature, to stop practising the art of duelling and to bring up pure pearls to the surface.)

Marx, that is, had expected clarity and a concrete rendering of the ideal from Hegel. The lack of clarity in the Hegelian rhetoric appears to have played some role in alienating Marx from the philosophy, of which he says he has only read fragments, and which he describes in the letter – as in the poem – as grotesquely rocky. Yet underneath the rhetoric were the sea of ideas and the dialectic which still attracted Marx. Thus, while he describes the dialectic in his epigram as having saved Hegel from drowning, Marx, the satirist, also ironically makes use of it to make an end of Hegel in his verse.

The image of the rock (later used to describe the Hegelian rhetoric in Marx's letter), characterises Hegel's dialectic in the first epigram and is, in the second epigram, the point from which both philosopher and poet fall:

> . . . For, as the poet from a roaring flood, toppling from the soaring
> rock,
> Envisages the words and thoughts of the beloved,
> And what he dreams recognizes, and what he feels envisages,
> So can each one suck the refreshing nectar of wisdom . . .

Ironically the persona's equation of poet and philosopher must give authority to Marx's satirical interpretation of Hegel's thought and parody of his dialectic: both in their way have 'sucked the nectar of wisdom'. The authority for the philosopher's wisdom is, however, made ironic in the last verse of the epigram, when the nature of his discovery, the Logos, is revealed as 'Nothing', 'ein Nichts':

> Alles sag' ich euch ja, weil ich ein Nichts euch gesagt!

> (I tell you everything, in telling you a Nothing!)

Just as 'the Word' had been made ambiguous in the second epigram, and its specific standard language meaning added to its symbolic sense in Epigram 2, so now 'Nothing' exists in the conclusion of the second epigram as a potentially ambiguous word, as both the 'sacred' negation of the negation in the dialectic, and the everyday emptiness of rhetoric. The dialectic was developed by Hegel in his *Science of Logic* according to the laws of the transformation and retransformation of quantity into quality, the law of the interpretation of opposites, and the law of the negation of the negation. Hence the negation of Being was Nothing, and that of Nothing Becoming. The contradiction to the laws of traditional logic offered by the concept of the negation of the negation (to the law that something cannot be both itself and its negation) is satirically foregrounded by Marx in both the epigrams and in *Scorpion und Felix*.

Later, in 1844, in the *Economic and Philosophical Manuscripts*,
Marx was to speak of the Young Hegelian Criticism being hopelessly
trapped within the idealistic Hegelian dialectic. According to this only
the publication of Feuerbach's theses in the *Anekdota* and of the
materialist criticism of the negation of the negation as the 'absolute
positive' had resolved the dilemma. Marx's own problem of releasing
himself from Hegel in the 1840s will be discussed in Part Two of this
study. The theological nature of the absolute positive is, as Marx goes
on to explain in 1844, also based for Feuerbach in its contradiction of
logic. In the epigrams of 1837 such a connection is not made and it
is the contradiction to logic alone, and not the idealism of the negation
of the negation which is satirised. In Chapter 39 of *Scorpion und Felix*
the dialectic is caricatured as both the 'writing on the wall' of a doomed
philosopher (the *mene, tekel, peres* facing Belshazzar which defied all
interpretation by his wise men), and as a Holy Trinity of nothings, of
'Nicht — Nichts — nicht'. Here it could be said that Marx attacks
Hegel's monism as 'negative' theology as well as its logical confusion,[15]
but it is from a Kantian and not a materialist standpoint that this attack
is made.

The full significance of the final verse of Epigram 2, 'Alles sag' ich
euch ja, weil ich ein Nichts euch gesagt', is only made apparent with
the reading of the following satire, the third epigram, which
ironically offers a synthesis of the 'Word', which had signified
certainty in Epigram 1, with the 'Nothing' of Epigram 2, which implied
return to confusion. The synthesis in Epigram 3 ironically appears in
the form of a positive, material 'Nothing', the filth of the streets:

> . . . But I only try to understand,
> What I found — on the street.

The German of the last verse, 'Was ich — auf der Strasse fand!' suggests
that the persona searching for truth on the street has found this in the
form of 'Kot' or filth, rather than in the form of gold. The person of
Hegel looking for the idea in reality is travestied as a fool's search.
Only in the letter of 10 November 1837 does Marx himself speak of
searching for the idea in reality as an Hegelian. The point of the
epigram makes it clear, moreover, that the 'realist' Hegel is guilty of the
same crime as that which he has accused Kant and Fichte of commit-
ting: of searching for and finding 'Nothing'. The Hegelian synthesis of
the ideal and the real (and his claim for the identity of opposites) is
condemned as being as equally negative, if not more so, than the

dualism of Kant's philosophy which it had opposed. By implication, and by turning Hegel's attack on Kant into an argument *ad hominem* against the speaker, Marx makes the persona into the target of satire and offers a defence of Hegel's targets of criticism, Kant and Fichte.

It is here that the function of Marx's initial vagueness on the identity of the speaker becomes clear; for it has served to maintain the ambiguity of the persona as both a voice and a target in the satires. It is this ambiguity of function which has misled several critics in their interpretation of the epigrams. But the ironic nature of Marx's 'identification' with Hegel through the use of the first person for the persona is foregrounded by the pseudo-apology given in the last epigram. Not only does Marx now ask pardon for the epigrams spoken with the voice of Hegel, but also implies that the filth of the street investigated by Hegel may be the product of the philosopher's own teachings: in terms of Hegel's system, the philosopher is shown viewing part of his own nature when looking at what he thinks to be the universal, the synthesis of mind and thought. Though Marx's epigrams show that he knew of Hegel's philosophy in 1837, they do not express admiration but criticism for the Berlin School.

Marx's use of the object of his satire as the voice of his epigrams follows a tradition practised by Erasmus in his *Praise of Folly* and in von Hutten's *Dunkelmännerbriefe, Letters of the Obscuranti*, of the Reformation, later to be used by Bruno Bauer in *Die Posaune* to defend the Hegelian Left in 1841. The *Letters of the Obscuranti*, attributed to von Hutten, were part of a literary hoax aimed at attacking the opponents of the rationalist Reuchlin by publishing letters attributed to them (the *obscuranti*) which placed absurdities in their mouths. It has been noted that Hegel, into whose mouth Marx was also to place absurdities in his epigrams, had been introduced in the opening epigram as a 'god swathed in darkness', an obscurantist rather than a rationalist. It was this theme of obscurity in the meaning of Hegel's philosophy which was elaborated on in the following epigrams, making both the subject and method of Marx's satire similar to those of von Hutten.

Marx's use of the epigram form here was — as with Marx's other epigrams — also modelled on classical example. Apart from giving the subject of satire in the title, the use of the pointed conclusion (as found also in the *Xenien* of Goethe and Schiller and in Heine's *Buch der Lieder*) relates Marx's epigrams to a classical model. Lessing (whose essay on art and poetry, 'Laokoon', Marx mentions reading)[16] had written in his 'Anmerkungen über das Epigramm',[17] that the epigram consisted of two parts: the *Erwartung*, or expectation, in which the curiosity of the reader for the subject is aroused, and the *Aufschluss*, the resolution or explanation, which may be pointed and come as a shock, or elicit laughter.[18] To achieve this effect the *Aufschluss* is often made only in the last verse. While this, as we have seen, is obviously the case in Epigrams 3 and 4, it is at first perhaps less obvious in the second:

I tell you everything, in telling you a 'Nothing'!

Yet in the context of the fourth, the first two epigrams can be seen as making – on this broader scale – the ironic Erwartung to the more satiric Aufschluss added by the interpretation of 'Nothing' as both confusion and filth. Applying this pattern to the whole of the group, the last image of Epigram 1 also becomes ambiguous in the context of the cycle: the image of Hegel (the dwarf) clinging on to the rock of certainty he has found amidst the sea of his thoughts (or troubles, if an allusion to *Hamlet* can be suspected) colours the picture as that of a drowning man. In this way Marx adds several levels to the poem: parody of the dialectic, mockery of the Hegelian rhetoric, and satire against Hegel's rejection of Kant and Schiller to search for the ideal in the real.

In summary it can be said, that in both form (as Schillerian satire contrasting reality with the ideal), and content (the defence of Kant and Fichte), the Hegel epigrams are based on the dualism of the real and the ideal later rejected in the letter of 10 November by Marx, and are 'realistic' only in an idealist sense.

Conclusion

In his *Anthropologie* Kant had praised the imitation of life in literature. Further to this he had, as we have seen, also named wit and parody as means to freeing the senses from preconceptions inhibiting the progress of reason. This is but one indication of the Kantian basis to Marx's use of satire in describing the reality of Berlin in order to compare it with a greater ideal, or to show it (in Kant's own words)[19] as being more 'limited' than the ideal.

In his adherence to Kantian ideas in his poetry, the young Marx differed from Heine, who, though he also acknowledged the importance of Kant in Germany's philosophical revolution, had been an interpreter of Hegel, since hearing him lecture in Berlin in 1822 on the philosophy of history.[20] Though we have seen that *Scorpion und*

Felix is still a work written from within Kantian Idealism, and Romantic in its use of irony to set up a series of mirrors to the author in his book, it also reveals a knowledge of the Young Germany 'silenced' in Marx's other poetic works. Here too the Kantian belief in the liberating power of Reason silenced the call to change the reality actually responsible for the writer's lack of freedom. In *Scorpion und Felix* we see the beginnings of Marx's rejection of Kantian aesthetics in the imitation and criticism of accepted ideals such as 'spiritualism' in writing. The relationship between Marx's use of parody in his early poetic works to the presence of the censor, as to the development of his explicit criticism of censorship, is the subject of Part Two of this study.

Notes

1. Several others have also taken this view as, for example, Robert Tucker (Tucker, p. 75). David McLellan and Peter Demetz are amongst the few to have argued that the epigrams are an attack on Hegel in defence of Kant and Fichte. Rüdiger Thomas also supports such a view in his essay 'Der unbekannte junge Marx' (1973), and disagrees with Günther Hillmann's *Marx und Hegel* (1966) that Marx's mentality was wholly Romantic at that time.
2. Nigel Reeves, 'Heine and the Young Marx' in *Oxford German Studies*, 7 (1973), p. 47.
3. Ibid., p. 52.
4. In *Journal of the History of Ideas*, April 1967, p. 259 f.
5. Ibid., p. 261.
6. Ibid.
7. Ibid.
8. Johnston, p. 263, is referring to the third of the economic and political manuscripts.
9. Ibid., p. 263.
10. Feuerbach's argument is explicitly put in the 'Vorläufige Thesen zur Reformation der Philosophie' in 1843. Kamenka writes in *The Philosophy of Ludwig Feuerbach*, London, 1970, p. 26, that Feuerbach's *Contribution to the Critique of Hegelian Philosophy* 'marked an unmistakable break with Feuerbach's Hegelian period', but this was in 1839.
11. Eugene Kamenka, *Ethical Foundations of Marxism* (2nd edn.), London, 1972, p. 23.
12. In *Varieties of Marxism*, Shlomo Avineri (ed.), Jerusalem, 1975.
13. Tucker, p. 57.
14. MEGA I/1 (2), p. 218.
15. MEGA I/1 (2), p. 86. Marx has just described Hegel as a 'dwarf', as, that is, a parody of the philosophical giants, one of these being Kant.
16. In his letter to the father of 10 November 1837.
17. In *Vermischte Schriften*, Berlin, 1771.
18. For Lessing, as for Kant, wit could serve as the embellishment to judgement and truth. Yet another Enlightenment satirist, Lichtenberg (known personally to Baron von Westphalen) might have served Marx as a model of

the epigram writer.
    19.   Kant, *Anthropologie*, p. 83.
    20.   Manfred Windfuhr suggests that Heine might even have heard Hegel's
lectures on the Philosophy of Religion in summer 1821, 'Heine und Hegel' in
Heine-Studien, Windfuhr (ed.), Düsseldorf, 1973, p. 265.

Part Two

FUNCTIONS OF PARODY IN THE EARLY WORKS OF MARX AND ENGELS

1   INTRODUCTION: PARODY AND MARX'S EARLY WORKS

The need for silence, created for the liberal writer by the censor, is one reason for the use of the 'underground languages' of parody and irony by Marx and his contemporaries in the 1830s and 1840s. These stylistic devices were, as Gutzkow had written in 1832, proven means of *Ideenschmuggel*, of 'smuggling' ideas past a censor. While irony enabled an author to conceal his intended meaning behind an apparent meaning, parody served both to mock other writers and to provide a 'word mask' for the parodist from the texts of his 'targets', behind which he could conceal his own aims. The more direct method of criticism, satire, could be used to confuse the censor by attacking a 'red herring' as a target in order to divert his attention to it and away from other more important opinions of the author. This was, however, a risky enterprise in view of the fact that a whole book could be banned for specific statements.

Problems with irony and parody, the other two ways of smuggling ideas past the censor, also became obvious to Marx. The cover of obscurity used by the parodist to conceal his meaning from the censor, also sometimes concealed his meaning from those very people he wanted to reach – the uninitiated. All too often parody served to restrict an author's message to a small group of those acquainted with the works being parodied and with the conditions creating the need for parody. Yet another drawback to the use of parody was that, if it were successful in silencing its target, it also created the possibility that a future audience not acquainted with the 'silenced' targets would not understand the point of the parody. Thus parody might be used to break the silence imposed on an author by the censor, or actively to silence other authors, but it might also inadvertently help to silence an author's criticism, by replacing direct issues or by restricting his readership to those able to read his text esoterically.

Heine had written in *Die Romantische Schule* (itself banned in 1835) that both Goethe and Cervantes had used irony to express views on their contemporary worlds and to avoid censorship. This was in itself Heine's way of ironically referring to the reason for his own need to use irony. His statement also gives a clue to the significance of the Young Germans' use of the figure of Don Quixote. But while their ambivalent sympathy with Cervantes's hero was born of their awareness of the role played by censorship in their own need to use irony, and in the creation too of naïveté in their public, Marx's use of the Don in his *German Ideology* of 1845-6, to satirise the idealism of Young Hegelians like Bauer, was related to his attempt to reject both naïveté in the reader, irony and other indirect forms of speech in the author and the censorship determining the perpetuance of those conditions themselves.

The Young Germans' and Young Hegelians' awareness of the need to read texts both esoterically and exoterically under a censorship which had forced meaning 'underground' into metaphor and irony had also, in cases such as Heine's and Bruno Bauer's, led them to read the exoteric, conservative Hegel 'esoterically' as a radical critic of the Prussian State. Yet in 1846 Marx saw that this rewriting of Hegel as a 'radical' only served further to chain the present to the past. Parody not only functioned as a means to attacking targets, but could limit one's own work to those targets. When too these objects of attack were successfully eliminated and had disappeared from the memory of the reading public, the attack itself, as we have just suggested, might not only become redundant but inaccessible to later readers. Apparently aware of all these limitations in the Young Hegelians' use of parody when he and Engels were writing the *German Ideology* (as when attacking the coterie nature of the readership of Young Hegelian works),[1] Marx himself nevertheless continued to use parody at great length in that work, as he had done earlier in *The Holy Family*. He used, as we will see, the structure and contents of the Bible satirically to imitate and mock the Young Hegelian use of Hegel's *Phenomenology of Spirit* as a Bible,[2] but also to criticise the idealist, and mystical, nature of their 'critical criticism'.

In combining biblical parody with an attack on the Young Hegelian use of Hegel's *Phenomenology* as a Bible Marx also showed himself to be a more radical interpreter of Hegel than the Young Hegelians, as well as a slightly more original utiliser of the biblical parody which they had often used to conceal what they considered radical from the censor.[3] By this means he juxtaposed their model with the means they had used to attack their targets to make it a target of parody, yet thereby he also, as we shall see, restricted his method of criticism, formally at least, to an imitation of theirs. In the case of *The German Ideology* parody also enabled Marx, as it had the Young Hegelians, to avoid censorship, in that it expanded the work to the statutory 20 and more publishers' sheets needed to avoid pre-censorship. But while at the same time it challenged the censor with its exaggerated blasphemies, it also

restricted Marx's audience largely to the objects of his attack, to the
Young Hegelians. Thus parody limited Marx to both the method of the
Young Hegelians and to the subjects of their criticism as his targets.
Bauer had earlier, in 1841, in his *Last Trump* (*Die letzte Posaune* über
Hegel . . .), used that device to speak of the 'esoteric' Hegel as a
revolutionary, under the ironically assumed mask of an imaginary
pietist enraged by Hegel's attack on the *status quo*. Marx had been
asked by Bauer to work with him on the continuation of that work,[4]
and it is known from a letter to him from Bauer, that Marx himself
planned a farce in 1840, entitled *Fischer Vapulans*. When, in 1844-5,
the attack by Marx and Engels on Bauer's *Critical Criticism* and his
journal the *Allgemeine Literaturzeitung* appeared with *The Holy
Family*, the critic Gustav Julias was quick to notice that the method of
'persiflage' used to attack Bauer imitated the 'Hegelian manner'.[5]

But in the same year another reviewer, in no. 87 of the *Frankfurter
Journal* (29 March 1845, page 2), criticised this use of persiflage as an
imitation of Bauer's own style which was no more than a way of
'fighting him with his own weapons':

> . . . Es ist gewiß an der Zeit, die 'absolute Kritik' der Bauerschen
> Richtung in ihrer ganzen Hohlheit zu zeigen; aber Marx hätte nicht,
> wie es hier geschieht, mit denselben Waffen kämpfen müssen . . .[6]

> (. . . It is certainly time to reveal the utter hollowness of Bauer's
> 'Absolute Criticism'; but Marx had no need, as he has done here, to
> fight them with their own weapons . . .)

Again, Marx's need to escape pre-censorship by publishing over 320
pages of an attack which was, originally, as he wrote to Feuerbach, to
have been a short pamphlet, must be kept in mind when asking what
functions the parody used in that work might have. Yet the above
criticism does point to Marx's dilemma of attacking Bauer in terms
understandable to him and other Young Hegelians, while at the same
time breaking from Bauer and from these terms themselves. Parody was
but one of the Young Hegelian weapons which Marx used to fight back
at them, from which, as the *Frankfurter Journal* suggested, he also
needed to break away. Yet, in psychological terms, the battle did, as
Marx claimed when speaking of the *German Ideology*, have the function
of *Selbstverständigung* — of understanding and coming to terms with
his past by working through it again from a critical standpoint. In this
sense parody also took on its old role, in carnival and literature, of

exorcising the past of the parodist, by turning that past into an object
of criticism. Yet a problem here was that parody was being used to
exorcise parody itself. Marx must have known Hegel's statement, made
in the *Ästhetik* read by Marx in 1837, that the 'parodic-satiric' form of
art was used by men to take up the past when they were ready to
oppose it. The dilemma facing Marx, of how to use parody to break
from a past which included the use of parody will be considered as a
central stylistic and epistemological problem facing Marx in the
German Ideology. It also requires to be put into the context of Marx's
use of parody from his early imaginative writings to the 1850s, and to
be related to the issue of censorship discussed in Part I of this study.

Very little has been written on the place of Marx's early imaginative
writings in either the literary or social context of their time. More place
has been given them in this biography, and they have often been misunderstood. A recent study by Reinhard Buchbinder[7] concentrates on
a stylistic analysis of Marx's use of the Bible in *The Holy Family* and
The German Ideology. Although it is in many ways a useful study, in
for example, giving references to many of Marx's biblical quotations
and parodies (a task which the editors of the new MEGA are also
undertaking), Buchbinder's work ignores many of the problems of
evaluating the function of Marx's use of biblical parody in 1844-6 in
his 'break' with the Young Hegelians in those works, by concentrating
on specific stylistic questions.

S.S. Prawer's erudite study, *Marx and World Literature*,[8] also
provides us with much useful information about Marx's literary sources,
but also without going into broader, related theoretical questions.
Peter Demetz's earlier work, *Marx, Engels und die Dichter*[9] (translated into English as *Marx, Engels and the Poets*), and Vera
Machackova's study of the imaginative writings of the young Engels,[10]
have also provided much useful information on a relatively obscure
corner of Marx studies.

This is not the place to give an extended review of the above literature, or to go over problems of Marxist aesthetics discussed elsewhere,
though many questions raised in Marxist aesthetics, such as that of
Marx's use of Schiller's concept of Art as play (in the *Paris Manuscripts*
of 1844), or of the concept of the fetish nature of art, shed interesting
light on the problems of art under the censor and of parody. It is the
aim of this brief study to point to some of the broader problems
surrounding Marx's use of parody which can be traced back to the
juvenilia or to the continued effects of censorship. Some, such as the
dilemma relating to Marx's attempts to use parody borrowed from

the Young Hegelians to break away from the Young Hegelian use of that method, have already been touched upon. Other related questions, such as the role of parody in the hypothesised 'epistemological break' which Louis Althusser suggested in 1965 had occurred in the 1845 works of Marx (but which he later moved to 1870),[11] will be discussed presently. To establish a context for the discussion of such questions, Marx's use of parody in early works such as *Scorpion und Felix* will be compared to his later application of the technique in the 1840s.

Parodie is defined in *Grimms Wörterbuch* (established in the nineteenth century) as the *Umbildung*, or 'reconstruction', of a known serious literary text into a comic work in which the form of the original is reproduced.[12] Though parody is given a satiric function in that definition, it is also attributed in this and other definitions the role of refunctioning older literary works for a new audience.[13] Its Greek root *para* is defined as meaning both 'beside' and 'opposite to', to indicate the ambivalence of some parody to its targets. This ambivalence − of nearness and opposition to a target − was embodied in Cervantes' *Don Quixote* for many nineteenth-century writers. Though the early German Romantics had also seen a tragic hero in the Don, and 'idealised' his idealism, the Schlegels' revaluation of the novel in the 1790s as a 'serious' comedy, also repudiated Gottsched's condemnation of satire as morally corrupting. Cervantean parody was enjoying a revival in the early nineteenth century in Germany, and two of its children, Fielding and Laurence Sterne − as well as the German writers, E.T.A. Hoffmann and Heine − were, as we have seen, taken up by the young Marx in 1837 as models for his fragmentary comic novel, *Scorpion und Felix*. As in *Don Quixote*, a function of parody in that work was to 'exorcise' the past. But whereas Cervantes was also attacking targets in his literary tradition known to a broad range of his readers, Marx's targets were those of his undergraduate reading. Thus the Roman law, Hegel, and religious history mix with allusions to Shakespeare, Goethe, and the Romantics.

In particular, allusions to Goethe abound in *Scorpion und Felix*. Not only is Felix the name of Wilhelm Meister's son, but references are made to other characters from that work such as Mignon, while we have (as we have seen) a grotesque caricature of *Faust*'s naive heroine, Gretchen, in the cook Grethe, as well as, possibly, an anagrammatic reference to Goethe, and an allusion to his critic and parodist Pustkuchen, the 'baker of puff-pastry'. Marx's intentions were often unclear: was he, for instance, parodying the distortion of Goethe's works created by Pustkuchen's spiritualising parodies of Goethe in

creating distortions of Goethe's characters, or only playing with
Goethe's works as spirits of his student past to be exorcised? The
latter would not seem likely in view of Marx's continued use of
Goethe's works (documented by S.S. Prawer),[14] though parodistic
references to reading too much Faust in school are made by the
'Mephistophelean Pertini' in the one Act of *Oulanem* included with
the poems for the father in 1837. It is perhaps the authorised Goethe
who is exorcised together with authority itself in the novel, and it is
an exorcism, which (like the carnival) was of temporary duration.
Even after Marx's rejection of the Young Hegelians' idealist
criticism in 1844-6, he continued to use Goethe, though as a foil to
contemporary writers whom he wished to satirise. Thus, in *Die großen
Männer des Exils* of 1852, Kinkel's imitations of Goethe are satirised
as unintentional parody: Goethe's greatness is used as a measure for
Kinkel's smallness, and as Prawer has pointed out[15] Marx goes back to
an epigram against Pustkuchen written by Goethe, to satirise Kinkel
as being – like Pustkuchen – another bad imitation of Goethe, when
he writes:

Hat doch der Walfisch seine Laus.
Kann ich auch meine haben.

Yet one other clue to Marx's purpose in giving a Sterne-like treatment to Goethe in *Scorpion und Felix* is to be found in Goethe's own
Wilhelm Meisters Wanderjahre (the true *Wanderjahre* which followed
the *falsche Wanderjahre* published by Pustkuchen between 1821 and
1828). In Book 8, Section 7, Goethe had written:

Yorick-Sterne war der schönste Geist, der je gewirkt hat; wer ihn
liest, fühlt sich sogleich frei und schön; sein Humor ist unnachahm-
lich und nicht jeder Humor befreit die Seele.

Marx had, of course, despite Goethe's warning that Sterne's humour
'could not be imitated', attempted such a task and, moreover, through
a humorous treatment of Goethe himself. This ironic use of Goethe
could be seen as a further confession of faith in the great writer. But
Marx himself admitted (in the letter to his father of 10 November
1837), that the humour of *Scorpion und Felix* had been forced.
The concluding chapter, referred to earlier, in which the dog
Bonifacius is given a purgative to free him of his unwanted ideas,
indicates, however, Marx's recognition of this failing in his novel at

the time of writing. For while the dog Bonifacius is itself a parodistic reference to a letter by the sainted Bonifacius in which he describes a certain frustrating task as making him like a barking dog unable to save his master's goods from theft,[16] it also, as stated earlier, borrows the idea of its parody from other works. So that while parody in *Scorpion und Felix* can be said to have the ambiguous function of imitating works otherwise out of the reach of Marx's talent, while also ridding the student Marx of the books he had had to study and read, it is also self-consciously without any new goal, and is followed by Marx's disavowal of his career as a writer.

Marx's use of parody in *Scorpion und Felix* appears, paradoxically, to reflect both a desire to imitate great literature (both parodistic and otherwise) and to liberate himself from the process of imitation. But it should also be noted that Kant had spoken of parody and satire in his *Anthropologie* as one of those forms of comic contrast necessary for freeing the reader from preconceived ideas. This is not an insignificant point, in view of Marx's continued use of parody in the 1840s to free himself and his readers from past methods and ways of thinking, and this will be taken up again presently. While the *Eighteenth Brumaire* shows Marx taking up Hegel's (and Heine's) point about the use of parody to free men from the historical past, it may also be argued that his earlier works reflect Kant's anthropological, or psychological concept of parody as a means to epistemological change. In the third part of his *Anthropologie* Kant had dealt with various forms of perception: such as (1) contrast; (2) newness; (3) change; and (4) transformation. These are for Kant methods of perception used to win new knowledge of the world. The comic is then characterised as a way of creating *contrast*, and the works of the parodists Fielding and Aloys Blumauer taken as examples of this art. Blumauer's travesty of Virgil was much discussed at the time, some claiming it was irreverent in treating Virgil the way it did. Fielding's parody of Richardson's *Clarissa* is described by Kant[17] as providing welcome laughter to liberate the reader from Richardson's too oppressive pathos. Here parody, as a form of comic contrast, is attributed a cathartic function by Kant. Yet when parody is (as in Marx's comic novel) only imitative of this cathartic function, this liberating effect cannot be assured. Similarly, Marx's parodistic imitation of Young Hegelian parody in the 1840s, when used to free himself from their methods, initially appears to fail in this task and leads to the eventual rejection of the method itself.

The reference made by Marx's father to Kant's *Anthropologie*, in his letter criticising one of Marx's poems as incomprehensible and

schwärmerisch is also best understood with reference to Kant's chapter
on originality (as opposed to imitation) in the use of the imagination.
There Kant distinguishes genius from the *Schwärmerei* in which
originality and sense do not, as with genius, harmonise. It is, however,
Schwärmerei which Marx's father had found in his son's poetry.
Though many of Marx's verses treat the subject of genius, it is clear
that Marx was himself aware of his failure to attain that goal in writing.
The imitation of parody in *Scorpion und Felix* may be seen as paying
homage to a Kantian ideal,[18] but in the awareness that it is out of
Marx's own reach. The ideals of wit, sagacity, and originality (or genius)
were for Kant the three talents acting in the discovery of knowledge.[19]
Marx's poetic works demonstrate a striving after all of these virtues,
while his letter of November 1837 acknowledges his failure to achieve
them. The parody used in *Scorpion und Felix* appears in an ambiguous
role, not only as the imitation and criticism of Marx's models, but also
as both following Kant's dictum to use wit to create new knowledge,
and expressing Marx's awareness of the epigonal character of his
imitation of parody and of its failure to create anything new. Even the
punning resorted to in *Scorpion und Felix* can be seen as reflecting this
awareness, and Kant had also written, that punning was a shallow form
of wit.[20]

   Thus, though Kant's *Anthropologie* had supported the poet Marx in
describing poetry as the highest of the arts, in praising wit and parody
and in providing him with much material for the subject matter of his
verse,[21] it also offered judgement on imitative and *schwärmerish*
writing which Marx eventually, at the end of 1837, was to turn against
his own poetry. He continued, however, in the face of censorship to
imitate the parody of his contemporary Hegelians in the 1840s in the
causes of satire as well as of new knowledge. This, and Engels' use of
parody in their works of the 1840s, will be looked at in closer detail in
the following sections.

Notes

   1.   Marx spoke, for example, in the chapter on Feuerbach in *The German
Ideology* of the closed nature of Young Hegelian disputes: 'They forget all other
nations, all real events, and the *theatrum mundi* is confined to the Leipzig Book
Fair and the mutual quarrels of "Criticism".' (Marx and Engels, *The German
Ideology*, Moscow, 1968, p. 53.) See also Shlomo Alvineri, *The Social and
Political Thought of Karl Marx*, Cambridge, 1968, p. 100. '. . . Bauer's Critical
School thus limits itself to emancipating consciousness, as if consciousness were

the real subject and man its mere predicate. Socially, this position also limits the relevance of the Critical School by definition to a small elite of literati, and prevents its identification with any universal postulate of mankind as such.'

2.   MEGA I/5, p. 135.

3.   Marx also puts eighteenth-century Rationalism's parody of the biblical word to attack theological orthodoxy to a new service, in using it to attack the Young Hegelian school as a new form of orthodoxy in philosophy. Leo Strauss, *Spinoza's Critique of Religion* (1930), New York, 1965, p. 143, writes that Lessing had believed that orthodoxy had to be 'laughed out of a position from which it could not be driven by any other means'.

4.   It is generally held that Marx never completed his part of Bauer's work and that Part Two of the *Posaune* was written by Bauer alone. In his study *Bruno Bauer and Karl Marx* (The Hague, 1977) Zwi Rosen suggests that this can be shown conclusively, and attacks Gustav Mayer's argument (in *Marx und der zweite Teil der Posaune*, 1916) that a case for Marx's authorship of the work could be made. But Bauer's use of irony and the continued existence of a reason for this irony – the censor – do make a conclusive answer to this problem difficult. Rosen tends to avoid this point, and also omits mention of Mayer's argument that Marx had both to write within the limits of Bauer's ironic style and to take into account the limits laid down by the censor. Marx's considerable talent for mimicry (demonstrated in his use of parody) must also not be left out of consideration in any 'textual analysis' aimed at deciding the authorship of the *Posaune II*.

5.   Julias wrote in Wigand's *Vierteljahrschrift*, 1845, vol. 2, pp. 326-33, reprinted in Wolfgang Mönke, *Die heilige Familie. Zur ersten Gemeinschafts- arbeit von Karl Marx und Friedrich Engels*, Glashütten im Taunus, 1972, p. 238:

> . . . Ganz artig ist die Persiflage, welche die genannten Herren als Waffe gegen die 'absolute Kritik' gebrauchen, indem sie diese letztere, in einer die Hegelsche Manier nachäffenden Weise, als kritischen Prozeß sich durch verschiedene Momente dialectisch entwickeln und auf jeder Stufe, in irgend einem Mitarbeiter der 'Literaturzeitung' zuletzt in Bruno Bauer selbst, sich gleichsam hypostasiren lassen . . .

6.   Mönke, ibid., p. 80.

7.   Reinhard Buchbinder, *Bibelzitate, Bibelanspielungen, Bibelparodien, theologische Vergleiche und Analogien bei Marx und Engels*, Berlin, 1976.

8.   S.S. Prawer, *Karl Marx and World Literature*, Oxford, 1976. Reviewed, M. Rose in *Quadrant*, October 1977, pp. 80-2.

9.   Peter Demetz, *Marx, Engels, und die Dichter*, Frankfurt-am-Main, 1969.

10.   Vera Machackova, *Der junge Engels und die Literatur*, Berlin, 1961.

11.   In short, Althusser's removal of the break from 1845 to the 1870 reduces the problematic of which the early works of Marx are said to be symptomatic to a few marginalia.

12.   *Grimms Wörterbuch*, vol. 7, p. 1464.

13.   The definition and theory of parody, was discussed in a workshop held in the Humanities Research Centre, Canberra in July 1976, papers from which will appear shortly.

14.   'Mephisto and Old Nick', in *Proceedings of the English Goethe Society 1975*, and *Marx and World Literature*, Oxford, 1976.

15.   'Mephisto and Old Nick', p. 46.

16.   See the new MEGA, I/1, Apparat, p. 1249. The concluding lines of *Scorpion und Felix* read:

'Armer Bonifacius! Deine heiligen Gedanken und Betrachtungen
verstopfen dich, seitdem du sie nicht mehr in Rede und
Schrift von dir geben kannst!'

'O! du bewunderungswürdiges Opfer von Ideentiefe, o du
fromme Verstopfung!'

17.   Kant, *Anthropologie*, p. 64.
18.   Michael Moering points out in *Witz und Ironie in der Prosa Heinrich von Kleists*, München, 1972, that while Kant sanctioned wit (*Witz*) as a hand-maiden to philosophical argument and to the growth of understanding, Friedrich Schlegel had defined irony as a form of philosophical wit, and Jean Paul had gone further in the *Vorschule* to an aesthetic of 1804 in defending it as being of primary importance in an aesthetic. Moering perhaps argues too strongly that Kant's 'relegation' of wit to a servant of philosophy had undermined it, in view of the Gottschedian tradition of condemning satire outright which preceded Kant's defence of wit and of parodists such as Fielding and Blumauer. It can also be argued that Jean Paul is dependent on Kant for the ideas developed in his aesthetic.
19.   Kant, *Anthropologie*, p. 164.
20.   Ibid., p. 166.
21.   Marx's father asks Marx whether he hasn't taken the subject for his incomprehensible poem from Kant's *Anthropologie* and Marx's preoccupation with the psychic states of *Wahnsinn, Zerrissenheit*, and genius is a preoccupation with themes discussed by Kant in his *Anthropologie*.

2.1 THE YOUNG ENGELS: POET AND PARODIST

Friedrich Engels (born in Barmen in 1820) had, as both Peter Demetz and Vera Machackova have shown, spent perhaps even more of his talents on poetry and satire in his youth than Marx. His early works were modelled on the extoric *Löwe — und Wüstenpoesie* of another Barmen poet, Ferdinand Freiligrath. As is the case with the collections of Marx's poetry, Engels' works contain both satires and parodies on contemporary subjects as well as more exotic and Romantic verses. Both groups also conform largely to Schiller's statement that elegy and satire were alternative (and equally *sentimentalische*, or Romantic) ways of contrasting reality to an absent or lost ideal. The second poem given by Riazanov in his edition of Engels' early works (MEGA 1/2), demonstrates, however, an attack on the false ideals of the Biedermeier which marks a more critical and realistic trend in Engels' works in 1839. The poem, *An die Feinde,*[1] was first published in *Der Stadtbote* of Bremen, on 24 February 1839, and then in the 'opposition' paper, the *Bremischer Unterhaltungsblatt.*[2] It begins and ends with a description of the ideal of honest endeavour, which it satirises, however, as being in danger of becoming an empty slogan. Such ideals were typical of the Bremen *Stadtbote*, and for three months or so the journal had published poems sent to it by Engels under the pseudonym of 'Theodor Hildebrand', never realising apparently that these poems were parodies of its own articles! Edited by Albertus Meyer (described by Riazanov as Bremen's guardian of morals), the Bremen *Stadtbote* was (as Engels implied in an article of July 1840),[3] a typical Biedermeier journal, written with little talent and much moralising.

In a letter to Wilhelm Graeber of April 1839[4] Engels himself describes how he sent poems to the *Stadtbote*, parodying their articles, and how he has put this revelation into another poem — a 'meta-parody', *To the Bremen Stadtbote*, describing the process of quotation and imitation, by which means the parodies had been made. The poem in question contains an excellent explanation of the mechanisms of parody, of how the parodist had taken his material from the object of his satire, the *Stadtbote* itself, turned its prose into verse and presented its target of satire with a mirror-image of itself. Unrecognised by its target, the parody had successfully mocked the journal's lack of insight into reality. In other poems Engels had also capitalised on the

fault of the *Stadtbote* which was to allow him to get away with his
hoax: exploiting the journal's lack of insight and intelligence which
enabled him to do little more than to copy out extracts from it to
satirise it. The poem *Bücherweisheit*, for example, had imitated the
empty moralising tone of the *Stadtbote*, to condemn its lack of
understanding in its glorification of the printed word:

> Der ist nicht weise, der aus allen Schriften
> Sich einen Schwall von Worten zugelegt, . . .
> Des Herzens Stimme, diese muss er hören,
> Und der geht unter, der sie hat verkannt,
> Von ihren Worten all, den inhaltsschweren,
> Das inhaltsschwerste heisst Menschenverstand.

Here the anonymous poet ostensibly condemns the wisdom born only
of books, arguing in his conclusion that the most meaningful word
must be *Menschenverstand*, common sense and understanding. In
printing the parody of its own style, the *Stadtbote* had proven conclusively its own lack of *Menschenverstand* and the truth of Engels'
parody.

To 'guy' the style of the *Stadtbote*, Engels' final 'meta-parody',
To the Bremen Stadtbote, was also written in an ironic moralising tone:

> Stadtbote, hör's, doch ärgre nicht Dich drüber,
> Wie ich zum Besten lange Dich gehabt;
> Denn merke Dir's, man spottet des, mein lieber,
> Der immer sich erzeigt als übergeschnappt.
> Dein blauer Freudenhimmel wird stets trüber,
> Nun Du ein Vierteljahr herumgetrabt,
> Was Du zu sagen, Edler, Dich beflissen,
> Das hast Du alles wiederkäuen müssen.

Its second stanza explains the process of parody, and plays ironically
around the idea of having taken its example from the journal:

> Ich nahm stets aus Dir selber meine Themata,
> Du hast sie alle selbst mir präpariert,
> Aus Deinen Reden machte ich Poemata,
> Darin ich Dich, allein Dich persifliert.
> Nimm Ihnen nur des Reims, der Metrik Schemata,
> So wird Dein Ebenbild Dir vorgeführet,

Nun fluch, beliebt es Dir vom Zorne wild entbrannt,
Auf Deinen ganz ergebnen
    Theodor Hildebrand.

The Lawrence and Wishart translation of this is somewhat free, but captures the spirit of Engels' verses. It reads:

To the Bremen Courier
Dear Bremen Courier,
    Please don't be offended
If you've become the laughing-stock of town.
Remember, friend, that folk have always tended
To ridicule what's patently unsound.
Your sunshine days have very nearly ended
In the three months that you've been trotting round.
Have you been saying things you didn't ought,
To give yourself such food for afterthought?

My poems cost little effort when I did them;
The donkey work was almost wholly done.
I took your articles and parodied them;
The subject-matter came from you alone.
Simply subtract the rhyme-schemes and the rhythm —
The image that remains is all your own.
Rage, if you like, at your respectful and
Obedient servant,
    Theodor Hildebrand.

The *Stadtbote* appears to have collapsed in April 1839 after only four months of publication. The power of parody as an effective tool of satire may have appeared to have been proven by his target's demise to Engels, and he continues to use parody to hold up a mirror to his enemies' faults, both in 1842 in *Der Triumph* when he attacks the pietist critics of Bruno Bauer, and in 1844 in *The Holy Family*, where he and Marx criticise the Bauer brothers themselves. In its context in the early works of 1839, parody, such as that used by Engels against the *Stadtbote*, appears, however, to have had the positive (or effective) function of freeing him from the type of Romantic satire used in earlier works such as *Die Beduinen*. Reality is no longer only compared to the ideal and found wanting; now the ideals of the Biedermeier are themselves put into question by being faced with their mocking distortion by the parodist. Although the value of ideals as such is not necessarily thereby put into question, the main subject of Engels' satire is now the false idealism of his age.

Engels could be said to have been influenced by both Gutzkow and Börne at this time, and he had also come into contact with works of the Young Hegelians. Demetz writes that in spring 1839 Engels had also read D.F. Strauss' *Das Leben Jesu*, and by winter 1840 had acquainted himself with Hegel's *Philosophy of History*.[5] In 1841 he was (like Marx) a member of the Young Hegelian club known as *Die Freien*, and had become acquainted with Ruge's *Halle Yearbooks*.

Engels' evaluation of Heine appears to have been complicated by his allegiance to Börne at this time. While Engels' *Brief aus dem Wupperthal* of 1839 still showed the influence of Heine's *Reisebilder*, and his essay on Arndt a certain sympathy with the anti-francophobic feeling of Heine's articles in the *AZ* (the *Augsburger Zeitung*), Engels expressly attacked Heine's answer to Gutzkow's biography of Börne made in *Ludwig Börne* in 1840. Only after their meetings (with Marx) in Paris in 1843 did Engels' attitude to Heine again begin to grow sympathetic, following, specifically, Heine's defence of the Silesian weavers which was published in 1844 in *Vorwärts*, and praised by Marx in a following number. Marx's continuing interest in Heine is to be found in the quotations from *Deutschland. Ein Wintermärchen* in *The German Ideology* written with Engels in 1845, and in *Die Grossen Männer des Exils* of 1852.

Yet another poem written around the theme of liberty after spring 1841 by Engels was *Nachtfahrt*, published on 3 January 1841 in the *Deutscher Courier*[6] under the pseudonym of Friedrich Oswald. Apparently written for the new year, the poem describes the anger felt at seeing freedom suppressed, as well as hope for a new dawn after the battle: 'wenn nah' der Morgen, drückt der Alp am meisten!', and in a poem describing the fall of the god Napoleon, entitled *Sanct Helena. Fragment*,[7] Engels compared the French general (as Napoleon himself had done in his letters from St Helena) to a modern Prometheus, now, however (like the fire he had stolen), a burnt-out candle. The themes of Engels' poetry in the 1840s — of freedom, the French Revolution, and Rationalism — were those of the Young Germany, whose history he had described in some detail in a letter to Friedrich Graeber of 8/9 April 1839.[8] There he had attacked the critics of Young Germany, the pietist Hengstenberg and the critic Wolfgang Menzel, making explicit his then recent change from pietism and Romanticism to the ideals of the Young Germany. One work which represents his allegiance to the

latter group, and which contains both parody and an attack on the
censor is his parodistic version of *Der gehörnte Siegfried*, a *Volksbuch*
or chap-book, described by Engels in his article 'Die deutschen
Volksbücher' of November 1839 as the most important of the chap-
books read by him, and as a mixture of poetry, naivete, and humorous
pathos.[9] In the 1840s Siegfried became for Engels a symbol of the
Young German revolutionary, and an alternative Messiah figure to the
aged Barbarossa and to the use of that myth for the revival of the old
Holy Roman Empire.

In a description of the Rhineland in the following year, Engels
visits Xanten, scene of Siegfried's exploits. Here Engels describes his
admiration for the character of the young hero:

> Was ist es, das uns in der Sage von Siegfried so mächtig ergreift?
> Nicht der Verlauf der Geschichte an sich, nicht der schmählichste
> Verrat, dem der jugendliche Held unterliegt; es ist die tiefe
> Bedeutsamkeit, die in seine Person gelegt ist. Siegfried ist der
> Repräsentant der deutschen Jugend.[10]

Siegfried's significance for Engels lies in his representation of German
youth, its desire for activity (*Tatenlust*) and for freedom. Engels'
travel sketch then turns (like the political travel sketches of the
Jacobin Georg Forster and of Heine's later *Reisebilder*) into an attack
on the restrictions put on youth, on censorship, and the righteousness
(as it appeared at the time) of the recent amnesty given by the King.
But unlike the admiration of Marx for Prometheus in 1837, Engels'
for Siegfried is expressed not only directly and in the use of the figure
as a political symbol, but also through its use in parody for the purpose
of literary satire in the *Fragmente einer Tragikomödie* (*Fragments of a
Tragi-Comedy*), *Der gehörnte Siegfried*.[11] Full of parodistic references
to other literary heroes,[12] Engels' *Gehörnte Siegfried* is a vehicle of
satire against the Biedermeier and its pietist critics. In defending the
Young Germany the work also finalises Engels' break with his pietist
background which had begun, as he had claimed, with his reading of
Freiligrath and which was completed with his reading of Young
Hegelians such as D.F. Strauss in 1841. Like Marx, Engels then commented on the new censorship instruction of 24 December 1841, but
unlike Marx Engels had already commented explicitly on the repressive
role played by the censor. *Der gehörnte Siegfried* gives us one such
example of Engels' early condemnation of the censor.[13] Significantly,
the condemnation is made under cover of literary parody.

In the scene 'Schmiede im Wald' Siegfried's master is giving
directions to his workers (amongst them Wolfgang Menzel) on how to
make new books from old. It is a parody of the story of Siegfried's
apprenticeship in sword-making, and covertly satirises the Biedermeier
critics as being engaged in the unwitting parody of the heroic activities
of the true Siegfried: symbol for the Young Germany, and for Engels
himself. Not only is the Biedermeier forging books where Siegfried
(the spirit of action) had forged a sword, but its books are written
against the new 'true' Siegfried, the Young Germany, and are,
moreover, plagiaristic. The advice of the Master Smith to borrow from
the old Romantics and from Goethe if there is not enough 'iron',
implies that the books of the Biedermeier lack both poetic and political
impact, but also reflect Engels' Börne-like dislike of the aesthetic
Goethe:

> Werft alles dann auf einen Kloss,
> Des Publikums Magen ist gar gross.
> Und habt ihr nicht des Eisens genug,
> Dafür weiss Rat der Meister klug;
> Drei Helden von Scott, drei Frau'n von Goethen,
> Ein Ritter von Fouqué, grimm und stählern,
> Mehr sind wahrhaftig nicht von Nöten
> Zu den Novellen von zwölf Erzählern!

The satire concludes with a mock battle between pietists and Hegelians,
which is to be repeated in Engels' satirical defence of Bruno Bauer in
1842. (The archetype of the mock battle in parody is the satiric
Batrachomyomachia, a parody of the Homeric epics.) Engels' attack on
the 'obscurantist' theologians Krummacher and Hengstenberg is also
symptomatic of his loss of faith in the Protestant orthodoxy of Bremen
and in the pietism of his childhood. In fighting for Bauer against the
pietist critics of radical Hegelianism in 1842 (and specifically against
Schelling), Engels progresses to a new perspective, yet while the tools of
his satire are not dissimilar from those used in 1842 by Bauer (and by
D.F. Strauss and other Young Hegelians), they also develop the
technique of parody used by him in 1839 to mirror the folly of targets
such as the *Stadtbote*.

Engels' development (late in 1839) away from the exotic
Romanticism of Freiligrath's *Löwe – und Wüstenpoesie* towards the
more realistic satire of the Young Germany was thus at the same time
a development towards his satiric use of parody in *Der Triumph des*

Glaubens of 1842 and in his contributions to *The Holy Family* in 1844.

Notes

1.   See *Marx/Engel Collected Works*, vol. 2, p. 5, for a translation of this poem.

2.   Machackova, p. 70, suggests that both papers published the poems thinking they parodied the other. Yet the poem's ambiguity may well have convinced the *Stadtbote* of its Biedermeier sentiments as being genuine.

3.   'Literatur', MEGA I/2, pp. 123-5.

4.   Ibid., p. 517. See also the letter to Engels' sister Marie of 12 February 1839, p. 580.

5.   Ibid., p. 29.

6.   MEGA I/2, p. 17 f.

7.   Ibid., p. 90; published November 1840.

8.   MEGA I/2, p. 502.

9.   Ibid., p. 51.

10.   MEGA I/2, p. 94. *Siegfrieds Heimat*, T.f.D., December 1840.

11.   Ibid., p. 507 ff.

12.   Ibid., p. 510.

13.   Another example is Engels' article for the *Telegraph für Deutschland* of November 1839 in which he condemns the lack of literary knowledge evident in the Prussian censor's choice of victims. Though his criticism had been made under cover of irony, Engels still expresses surprise that the relatively liberal Hamburg censor had allowed his criticism to be printed. (See letter of 9 December 1839 to Friedrich Graeber.)

2.2 PARODY IN THE STYLE OF BAUER: DER TRIUMPH DES GLAUBENS

In 1842 a work entitled *Die frech bedraüte, jedoch wunderbar befreite Bibel. Oder: Der Triumph des Glaubens* was published in Neumünster near Zürich by F.R. Hesse, later the publisher of the *Deutsch-Französische Jahrbücher*. The full title of the work suggested a parody of the chap-book of Dr Faustus from the early sixteenth century, as well as of Klopstock's late eighteenth-century pietistic epic, the *Messias*:

> Das ist: Schreckliche, jedoch wahrhafte und erleckliche
> Historia von dem weiland Licentiaten Bruno Bauer,
> wie selbiger vom Teufel verführet, vom reinen Glauben
> abgefallen, Oberteufel geworden und endlich kräftiglich
> entsetzet ist.
> Christliches Heldengedicht in Vier Gesängen.

The title tells the story ('terrible but true') of the one-time licentiate Bruno Bauer, how the same was seduced by the devil away from the true faith, grew to become a top devil and was finally powerfully overthrown. The final verse describes it (with a parodistic reference to Klopstock's epic) as a 'Christian epic poem in four cantos'. Bauer, at this time one of the more radical Young Hegelians, friend to Marx, and recently prevented from taking a new university post, is defended by Engels under the ironic pretence, or mask, of a pietistic attack on his radicalism. As in the case of Bauer's own ironic defence of the radical Hegel in his *Last Trump*, Engels also uses the mask of a pietist critical of the philosopher's radicalism to prove Bauer radical.

Engels' substitution of Bauer's name for that of Faust in his satire (as in the title above) creates an effect of incongruity which is also an indication of the parody which is to follow. Written in imitation of the style of pietist verse (once written by the boy Engels himself), the parody purports to condemn Bauer (who had been a theologian before turning to philosophy) as a Christian who has sold his soul to the devil. The real purpose of the 'hoax' — to defend Bauer against his pietist critics — (which Engels also does in the manner of the Reformation satirist von Hutten's *Letters of the Obscuranti*) is all the more obvious for the parody being an imitation of the parodistic style used by Bauer himself in 1841 to defend the radical Hegel in the work entitled *Die Posaune des jüngsten Gerichts über Hegel den Atheisten und Antichristen.*

The title of Engels' satire, *Triumph des Glaubens*, is also reminiscent of a farce written in 1817 by the Graf von Platen, entitled *Sieg der Gläubigen (Victory of the Believers)*, which had satirised orthodox theology and revelation. Yet Engels, despite the many literary allusions in the parody, takes his satire out of literary tradition and places it in the centre of a philosophical debate.[1] Engels had entered a debate on Schelling's opposition to the Left Hegelians in March 1842 with his essay 'Schelling und die Offenbarung', and had continued it with a satirical article of May 1842 entitled 'Schelling, der Philosoph in Christo, oder die Verklärung der Weltweisheit durch Gotteswisheit. Für Gläubige Christen, denen der philosophische Sprachgebrauch unbekannt ist'. The work is addressed, ironically, to 'believing Christians, to whom philosophical terminology is unknown': not only does Engels satirise the pietist reader's ignorance of philosophy, but implies that Schelling himself had not understood philosophy. The title also parodies the style of pietist essays, introducing the author in the guise of a pietist 'believer'.

Engels' ironic use of parody, similar in form to Marx's use of Hegel as both the voice and the target of his satiric epigrams of 1837, was clearly popular with the Young Hegelians at this time. Not only Bruno Bauer in 1841, but D.F. Strauss, in an earlier attack on Bauer, had used this form of ironic identification with the object of his criticism. On this piece of history Franz Mehring has written[2] that D.F. Strauss, whose *Leben Jesu* of 1835 had caused what has been called the 'first crack' in the system of the Old Hegelians, had been attacked by Marheineke and his disciple Bauer who were editing Hegel's *Philosophy of Religion*. Strauss had then seen Neander's parodistic *Frommes Leben Jesu* published against him as part of a pietist attack on his *Leben Jesu*. According to Mehring Strauss had given Neander's work the ironic motto, 'Ich glaube, Herr, hilf meinem Unglauben'. This parody of the pietist's prayer – 'I believe, Lord, help my disbelief' – characterises the pietist as a 'believer', whose lack of belief in Reason is, however, the real disbelief which will close heaven on earth to him. The title of Engels' *Triumph of Faith* refers to a tradition of lampooning pietist attacks on Rationalism in the writings of the young Hegelians. For this reason, attempts to interpret the work in isolation from those other satires of the Young Hegelians may miss some levels of irony in the satire,[3] as well as the essentially 'private' and limited nature of many of its statements. One of the problems with Engels' satire of 1842, and with the parodistic and satiric passages in *The Holy Family* of 1844-5 is their dependence on now forgotten material for the meaning of many of their allusions.

Strauss's counter-attack on Bauer had included an ironic comparison of himself, Strauss, when confronted with the mysteries of Bauer's logic, to Faust in the witches' kitchen of *Faust 1* listening to sounds 'like those of a hundred thousand fools!'[4] Strauss also compared Bauer's speculative arguments to those of the pietist Hengstenberg, which drove Bauer to reply in autumn 1839 with his *Beitrag zur Kritik des religiösen Bewusstseins*. At the same time, Engels (though not yet a member of the Freien where he was to meet Bauer and other Young Hegelians) attacked the conservatism of the pietists Hengstenberg and Menzel in their roles as the critics of the Young Germany movement.[5] One month later (in May 1839) he described reading the rationalists' and D.F. Strauss's 'criticisms of the Bible'. Strauss's work must be attributed a significant role in Engels' final break with pietism, especially as it is in this letter that he announces that he is no longer an orthodox believer in the literal truth of the Bible.

By 1841 the battle between Strauss and Bauer appears to have been overshadowed by Bauer's move to the left wing of the Hegelians. The terms 'left' and 'right' had been derived from D.F. Strauss's designation of those who believed totally or only partially in his thesis that the New Testament was historical. The nomenclature was later applied to other issues of Hegelian philosophy, but for Strauss Bauer's early defence of miracles (as well as his attack on Strauss) had placed him to the right of the centre. By 1841, however, Bauer had moved to the Left Hegelians. Bauer's defence of the 'esoteric' radical Hegel, and of his own alleged atheism (after this move to the left in the Hegelian school) was published anonymously in November 1841 in *Die Posaune des jüngsten Gerichts über Hegel den Atheisten und Antichristen* (*The Trumpet of the Last Judgement over Hegel the Atheist and Antichrist*).[6] Mehring describes how many (including the Young Hegelian Ruge, editor of the *Halle Yearbooks*) were at first hoaxed by Bauer's use of the mask of the enraged pietist, and thought it to be another attack on Hegel.[7] Bauer's use of the targets of his satire as the mask for his persona — this being the conservative outraged by Hegel and the Left Hegelians — was similar to the technique common amongst satirists of the Reformation, such as von Hutten, and had, as Marx's use of it in 1837 indicates, enjoyed a new popularity in the nineteenth century following the end to the eighteenth century's denigration of satire under Gott-sched's directives.

The technique was one, which (as Marx's epigrams have shown) could be used by a satirist defending old established forces against the new, as well as by rebels introducing new concepts to their readers. In 1840, before the publication of Bauer's *Posaune* (*The Last Trump*), Marx had apparently been working on a parody which would fall into the second category: it was his attack on the conservative K.P. Fischer's justification of theism, *Die Idee der Gottheit*, known as *Fischer Vapulans*. In the letter of 1 March 1840, referred to earlier, Bauer had written to Marx: 'Der Wisch von Fischer is jämmerlich elend. Was macht deine Farce: Fischer Vapulans?' Bauer had also commented that the philosophical scene in Berlin was now as interesting as politics were in other countries. The latter remark might also be taken as evidence for Bauer's belief that his Hegelianism was more effectual than political criticism, and as indicating that he expected Marx's farce to be a philosophical critique in parodistic form in the style of the farce he was to publish in 1841.

As early as April 1840[8] Engels had condemned K.E. Schubath's 1839 analysis of Hegel's *Staatslehre* as an example of the conservative reaction of the time to the Hegelian 'revolution'. Lucio Colletti, in his Introduction to *Karl Marx. Early Writings,*[9] writes that Engels' 1842 pamphlet on Schelling and Revelation ('Schelling und die Offenbarung') expressed the attitude to Hegel current amongst the 'young radical Idealists of the Berlin *Doktorklub*'.[10] This attitude, more complex than that put forward by Engels in 1840, was that 'there was a contradiction in Hegel between his revolutionary principles and his conservative conclusions'. This was, generally speaking, the argument put forward by Bruno Bauer in his revelation of the 'esoteric' Hegel in *Die Posaune* of 1841. As Colletti points out, this position prevented Bauer, Engels, and other Young Hegelians from recognising the more radical break with Hegel made by Feuerbach. Colletti also maintains that in 1842, when Engels is still within the school of Bauer, 'Marx had come under Feuerbach's influence and already assumed a clearly materialist position', and, further on,[11] that there is no evidence that Marx had accepted the idea of the radical idealist left, that there was a contra-diction between Hegel's radical principles and his conservative system. Colletti does not take issue, as this argument appears to suggest he should, with the claim that Marx had planned a sequel[12] to Bauer's *Posaune* in which this idea was suggested. Marx's planned sequel to Bauer appears from its title, 'Hegel's hatred against religious and

Christian art and his disbanding of all positive Laws of the State', to
have been another ironic defence of the 'esoteric' revolutionary Hegel
in the style of Bauer's *Posaune*. Marx's *Critique of Hegel's Doctrine
of the State* appears only in 1843. The Feuerbachian position suggested
by Colletti to have been Marx's, that criticism of Hegel made outside
rather than from within the Hegelians was the truly radical position
(more radical, that is, than the Young Hegelians' defence of the esoteric
Hegel) is explicitly put in *The Holy Family*, sub-titled 'Or Criticisms
of the Critical Critique'.

Bauer's *Posaune* is thought by Machackova[13] to have been the model
for Engels' satirical essay on Schelling of May 1842. Yet the essay also
contains a specific parody of an old target of Engels' satire, the pietist
F.W. Krummacher. In pretending to prove that Schelling was a good
Christian, the voice of Krummacher argues that Schelling was in fact no
philosopher. Thus Engels satirises both Schelling and the 'typical
pietist' through Krummacher. Machackova suggests that parody, with
its use of humour, enabled Engels to broaden his audience beyond that
of the Young Hegelians. While this may have been so in the cases of
some readers, the polarising effect of parody on an audience already
aligned with certain beliefs cannot be overlooked. Engels' use of an
ironic type of parody to insinuate the parodist into the camp of his
target (such as Schelling, or Hegel's pietist critics) appears to represent
an attempt to prevent this polarising effect from occurring as an initial
reaction in the reader, but it may also have restricted understanding
of the work.

It was in *Schelling und die Offenbarung*[14] that Engels had written
of Bauer's *Posaune* that it was a vindication of Hegel,[15] and Riazanov
notes that the attacks on Schelling were written by Engels at the same
time as the satirical epos *Der Triumph*.[16] Engels had already used
parody against Schelling, and (as we have seen) had several literary
parodies to his name, or at least to the pseudonym of 'Theodor
Hildebrand'.

The title of Engels' satirical defence of Bauer also parodistically
imitated not only the chap-book of Dr Faustus but the title of the
Lutheran Bible:

Die frech bedräute, jedoch wunderbar befreite Bibel.
Oder: Der Triumph des Glaubens.[17]

(The rashly threatened, yet miraculously 'freed' Bible.
Or: The triumph of faith.)

The subject of the work is already clear from its parodistic title, while its blasphemous levity marks the satire as an attack on orthodoxy rather than as a defence. Furthermore, ironic ambiguity is built into the title referring to the 'liberation' of the Bible, as the phrase 'befreite Bibel' contains the name of Bauer's radical club *Die Freien*. Thus the liberation of the Bible may (for the orthodox) be from *Die Freien*, but it is also a liberation for Bauer and *Die Freien* from the tyranny of orthodox theology.[18]

It is perhaps ironic that while Engels imitates a tradition of satire used by Bauer to attack the conservative opposition to a 'radical' reading of Hegel, he also uses Goethe's *Faust* as one of the vehicles of his attack, making the figure of Faust into a persona for Bauer himself, though it had earlier been used by D.F. Strauss to attack Bauer when the latter was on the right of the Hegelians. But, in general, Engels' equation of Bauer with Faust is an ironic caricature of the pietists 'damnation' of Bauer.[19] Faust is thus on the one hand the symbol of the damned soul and on the other an image of the Promethean: the 'two souls' in Faust's breast also serve to symbolise the ambiguity of Bauer's position, supported by the Hegelians and condemned by the pietist. In *Der Triumph des Glaubens* the battle for Faust's soul between God and the devil which opens *Faust 1* is thus transformed into a battle between pietists and Left Hegelians for the soul of the philosopher Bauer. Liberal quotation from Goethe's *Faust* is continuously used to satirise the pietist's opposition to Bauer through being parodistically turned into a defence of Rationalism against Deism. For example, in Engels' satire the Lord speaks in the metre of Goethe's *Faust* — yet is made to argue in a way foreign to Goethe's work, that Bauer's soul will be saved when he loses his reason:

> Und wenn er jetzt auch noch zu denken sich erkühnt,
> Verlass dich d'rauf, bald soll er die Vernunft verlieren.

Ironically, God appears not to be on the side of his hero in Engels' parodistic satire, but to be the pietist's advocate. In following verses Bauer's change from theology to philosophy is ironically paralleled to Faustus', and the opening monologue of Goethe's *Faust* changed accordingly:

> Da hab' ich nun, weh mir Phänomenologie,
> Ästhetik, Logik und Metaphysik
> Und leider auch Theologie

Durchaus studiert, nicht ohne Glück!

Bauer is ironically presented as not being too dissatisfied with his success in theology. But then, under the mask of the pietist, the author describes Bauer as having been seduced from that theology by Hegel. Hegel's horde of 'devils', consisting of French revolutionaries, the Berlin *Freien*, and other radicals, similarly reflect the pietist's view of these groups as 'devilish'. The mask of the pietist, the description of Bauer as a daemonic revolutionary, and the happy end in which good triumphs over the Revolution, all mirror satirically the prejudices of Bauer's enemies.

The comic effects of Engels' identification of Bauer with Faust rests in the similarity between the fiction imitated and the contemporary reality with which it is compared, as much as in the anachronistic juxtaposition of the contemporary philosopher with the legendary alchemist. In this, as in changing the perspective from that of the Left Hegelians to that of the persona of the pietist, the satire is ironic and often ambiguous. The loss of Bauer's soul may be interpreted as a victory from the point of view of the atheistic satirist, though from the point of view of the pietist, it is described as Bauer's tragic downfall. This ambiguous reaction is based in the nature of the 'bet' or wager between the Lord and the devil for Bauer's soul, by the terms of which Bauer must give up reason to preserve his soul. When Bauer does not, the Lord ironically must lose his bet to the devil, so that not only is the case of the rationalist satirist upheld against the pietist, but the pietist's authority, the Lord, is defeated by the devil. Engels has turned Goethe's *Faust* and the theology of the pietist on its head to make the one fit the other. For only a distorted 'Faust' can serve the pietist's purpose. The unity of Faust's striving for greater knowledge with the over-all plan of the Lord for his universe of Goethe's *Faust* is destroyed in Engels' parody, but this destruction is seen as a necessary result of the pietist's use of the Faust story to condemn Bauer and the philosopher's search for truth through reason. Though Bauer is brought to Hell, it is a hell ruled by Hegelians, and as this makes it clear that the Lord has lost his wager, the pietists' subsequent loss of his authority makes their victory over Bauer appear uncertain. Bauer (and the satirist)[20] may in fact, have won. Ruge and other members of *Die Freien*, who are shown as devil's men returning to the Lord for fear of the censor, are, on the other hand, shown to have joined the 'losing' side. Engels and Edgar Bauer remain amongst the radicals, the 'Montagnards' of Hell, defending Bauer, the Robespierre of the Revolution. This work ends in a parody of the Apocalypse with Bauer holding, appropriately, the *Posaune*, the trumpet of the Last Judgement, up against the four evangelists and their dubious 'triumph of faith'. In *The Holy Family*, two years later, it is Marx and Engels who hold their 'last judgement' on Bauer, but in a parody of the biblical rhetoric satirised by Bauer as well as of Bauer's own parody.

In *Der Triumph des Glaubens* in 1842 we see Engels putting parody to a new use, in at least the context of his own work, in the cause of philosophical ideas. Yet again Engels is imitating an existing tradition, found in the parody used in the disputes of the Young Hegelians and, as with the young Marx's use of parody, Engels' parody is not yet dialectical or innovative. This too, it will be argued, is the problem besetting the use of parody in *The Holy Family* of 1844-5. Only in 1845-6 do the joint writings of Marx and Engels begin to show a new critical approach to their use of parody and a way out of the incestuousness of the Young Hegelian use of parody. The ambivalent role of parody there as both a product of Young Hegelian critical method and as a way out of this method will be the subject of the following chapters.

Notes

1.   In a letter of 26 July 1842 Engels, who had not attended university as had Marx, wrote to Ruge that he was giving up his literary activities to study philosophy.

2.   Franz Mehring, *Aus dem literarischen Nachlass von Marx und Engels*, vol. 1, p. 20.

3.   The question of interference between the parodist's text and the model imitated by him which occurs when the parodist quotes not directly from the model but from another work which has imitated the model, has been touched upon in discussing Marx's juvenilia. I have also dealt with the topic in relation to Heine's parody of the Bible in *Die Parodie: Eine Funktion der biblischen Sprache in Heines Lyrik*, Meisenheim, 1976.

4.   Mehring, p. 30: 'Strauss meinte, in seinen Streitschriften, bei Bauers abentheuerlichen Deduktion sei ihm zu Muthe, wie dem Faust in der Hexenküche, als höre er ein ganzes Chor von hunderttausend Narren sprechen.'

5.   MEGA I/2, p. 502. Letter of 8/9 April 1839.

6.   Reprinted in Karl Löwith (ed.), *Die Hegelsche Linke*. The work is often referred to in English (as, for example, by David McLellan) as *The Last Trump*. Although Marx mentions working on a sequel, there is little concrete evidence to support the view that he had collaborated with Bauer on *Die Posaune* itself. Although a brief caricature of Marx appears in Engels' *Der Triumph*, no mention is made there of Marx as co-author with Bauer.

7.   Franz Mehring, *Karl Marx. The Story of his Life*, London, 1966, p. 33. David McLellan writes in *The Young Hegelians and Karl Marx*, London, 1969, p. 52, that the *Posaune* was first attributed to Feuerbach, who denied it,

complaining that he would not have written a defence of Hegel at this time. In a letter to Ruge of 6 December 1841 Bauer complains that Riedel's *Athenäum* had been foolish enough to reveal the *Posaune* as parody and Bauer as its author. MEGA I/1 (2), p. 264.

8.   In *Requiem für die deutsche Adelszeitung*, MEGA I/2, p. 72.

9.   *Karl Marx. Early Writings*, Colletti (ed.) (transl. R.S. Livingstone and G. Benton), Middlesex, 1975, p. 11.

10.   In *Der Triumph* of 1842 Engels mentions 'Die Freien'.

11.   Colletti, p. 13.

12.   The sequel was at first to be called 'Hegels Hass gegen die religiöse und christliche Kunst und seine Auflösung aller positiven Staatsgesetze'.

13.   Machackova, p. 253.

14.   MEGA I/2, p. 188, Engels writes of Schelling, that he had tried to smuggle 'belief in authority, pietist mysticism, and gnostic *Phantasterei* into the free science of thought'.

15.   Ibid., p. 185.

16.   'Der Triumph' appears to have been the last of the works written.

17.   Ibid., p. 253.

18.   The Enlightenment writer and critic Lessing had for some years continued an argument with the orthodox Pastor Goeze on the 'liberation' of the Bible from the words which orthodox theology regarded as too sacred to change.

19.   The pietist's condemnation of Faust had, as we have seen, been parodied by Marx in 1836 in his satires on Pustkuchen.

20.   Klaus Lazarowicz has pointed out in his study of satire, *Verkehrte Welt*, Tübingen, 1963, p. 1, that critics in the eighteenth century such as Mecke and Liscow had thought satire itself a creation of the devil. The theme is taken up in nineteenth-century works such as Grabbe's *Scherz, Satire, Ironie und tiefere Bedeutung.*

PARODY IN *THE HOLY FAMILY*: TOWARDS AN EPISTEMOLOGICAL BREAK?

In the Introduction of March 1965 to the English translation of *Pour Marx*[1] Louis Althusser designated *The Holy Family* an 'early' work in Marx's *oeuvre*, and *The German Ideology* as a work of the 'break'. As mentioned previously, Althusser has recently, in his *Essays on Self-Criticism* revised much of his early work, and moved the break to 1870, undermining, as also suggested earlier, much of his argument for a symptomatic reading. Althusser's contentious use of Bachelard's concept of the 'epistemological break' for Marx's work in his works of 1965 will be discussed in the following section. This chapter assumes as a whole, however, that Althusser's original designation of *The German Ideology* as a work of the break may be viable — having in any case been made on the basis of Marx's own designation of the work as one in which the change from philosophy to 'scientific' historical material-ism is evident — but that the concept of the break must be clarified further. It will also be argued in this chapter that the considerable use made of parody as a means to the criticism of speculative criticism in *The German Ideology* be seen in the context of this break. *The Holy Family* of 1844-5 will also be put into this context, in that it too makes use of parody as a means to the criticism of Young Hegelian thought, but without making any evident change to the terminology or methods of that school. Detailed analysis of specific examples of biblical parody in that work has been made by Buchbinder, but the aim of the follow-ing discussion is to consider how Marx and Engels develop their use of parody in the 1840s and how their use of it becomes both contra-dictory to their aims and limiting of them.

Both the first four chapters of *The Holy Family*, written by Engels, and those chapters written by Marx, make use of parody, imitating, if not quoting from the works of their target Bruno Bauer before distorting and juxtaposing the quotations with other statements. Superficially at least, the parody used in *The Holy Family* appears to differ from that used by Marx and Engels in their juvenilia. One obvious change is not so much in the method as in the object of analysis. While in Marx's *Scorpion und Felix* the subject of parody had been the philistine's misunderstandings and maltreatment of great texts, the object of satire in *The Holy Family* is the *Allgemeine*

Literaturzeitung edited by the 'holy family' of the three Bauer brothers, and, in particular, the 8th volume attacking the lack of *Geist* or spirit in the theory of the German communists. But, as with Engels' earlier use of Bauer's method of parody as a way of defending one philosophical position against another, the use of parody in *The Holy Family* is not innovative, but imitates a method practised by the target of its attack. This may be one factor in the failure of *The Holy Family* to produce any new alternative method to Bauer's 'speculative criticism'. Not only did Marx and Engels make no change to the Young Hegelian style of their work in *The Holy Family*, but the target of their attack, Bauer's journal, had collapsed a month before the publication of their criticism. Although Marx and Engels had, so to speak, set out to 'hoist Bauer with his own petard', by using his same method of biblical parody to attack him, the argument of their work implies they had also wanted to avoid being thus restricted to Bauer's methods. *The Holy Family* (and parts of *The German Ideology*) are symptomatic of a dilemma facing Marx at that time of finding both a new terminology and a theory to escape the mistakes of their target, the speculative criticism of the Young Hegelians. The 'crisis' created by this dilemma is exemplified in the way the use of parody in these works entrenches Marx and Engels in the very method and terminology they are attacking. The relationship of this 'crisis' to an 'epistemological break' in Marx's work, and the role of parody played in creating the former – if not the latter – is a central question to be treated in these concluding chapters, in the analysis of *The Holy Family, The German Ideology* and the *Eighteenth Brumaire*.

The language of the Lutheran Bible had often been used as a basis for political discussion in Germany (from Thomas Münzer to Wilhelm Weitling) as it had wide distribution amongst all classes of the population. Yet the use of biblical parody in Young Hegelian satires such as Bauer's *Posaune* and Engels' *Triumph*, to mock the pietistic interpretation of texts, appears rather to have had the effect of limiting their audience to those conversant with the arguments of the Young Hegelians. Parody had almost become a *franca lingua* amongst the group, being a method used to criticise each other as well as their enemies and, as a form or ironic self-quotation, had often resulted in obscuring the meaning of their arguments. The use of biblical language in *The Holy Family* produces a similar effect, for its purpose is not to satirise the pietist but to mirror the theological nature of Bauer's speculative criticism, as well as to mock Bauer's own use of biblical parody and biblical language in the criticism of the *Literaturzeitung*.

Even before the premature demise of that journal, *The Holy Family*
had been doomed to a certain redundancy, or at least to a limited
audience, in making the sense of many of its arguments dependent on
the reader's accurate knowledge of the articles of the Bauers' journal.
As we shall see, this danger had been recognised by the more hesitant
of the two critics, Engels, who believed the length of the book
(necessary for it to escape pre-censorship) to be out of proportion to
its matter.

To Marx Bauer's 'Kritische Kritik' was the distorted reproduction of
Hegel's *Kritik* and of speculative Idealism, and parody served to mirror
the nature of Bauer's criticism as caricature. Specifically, Marx
attacked the conservative attitude taken by Bauer in the *Allgemeine
Literaturzeitung* of 1844 following the censorship of Bauer's more
radical writings.[2] Bauer's attitude to censorship was, however, as Heft,
6 (p. 38 ff) shows,[3] explicitly critical; it was his attack on Feuerbach's
sensualism and (in the August issue of the journal) his criticism of the
so-called lack of 'spirit' in communist philosophy, which won him
no sympathy from Marx at that time. Marx argued that Bauer's idealism
prevented him from giving any effective critique of the censor, as, in
Bauer's philosophy, the latter must always appear internalised in the
mind of the critic, and, hence, as a figment of his imagination.

In their counter-attack Marx and Engels turned to parodying the role
assumed by *Geist* or spirit in speculative idealism. The Preface, written
in Paris in September 1844, speaks of the threat to *der reale
Humanismus* from *der Spiritualismus oder der spekulative Idealismus.*
The subject of this *realer Humanismus* is described as being 'the real
individual person' and not spirit. Despite the use of Feuerbachian
categories to oppose Bauer's speculative idealism, the contrast between
realism and idealism and the equation of spiritualism with idealism
remains abstract. In this the work differs from *The German Ideology*.
Although critics such as V. Adoratskij (the editor of the MEGA volume
of *The Holy Family*, MEGA I/3), have written that Marx's and Engels'
attack on Hegelian idealism in the work of 1844-5 laid the foundation
stone of 'revolutionary-materialist socialism', and that Marx in 1867
was not (despite the work's Feuerbachisms) ashamed of it, from the
point of view of the purpose of an analysis of the functions of parody
in the transformation of the language of idealism, *The Holy Family*
does not offer in its Preface or in its parodistic passages evidence of a
radical break in style from its target Bauer.

Franz Mehring has republished the correspondence between Marx
and Engels on the writing of *The Holy Family* in the second volume of

his work *Aus dem literarischen Nachlass von Karl Marx und Friedrich Engels.*[4] The majority of remarks from Engels contain surprise at the length of the work. In his letter of 20 January 1845 he comments on how Marx has extended the work to twenty publishers' sheets (the number required for a work to avoid pre-censorship). As only one and a half of these sheets, the first four chapters, were written by Engels, he felt that his name should therefore not be put first before Marx's on the title page, especially as the publisher's new title, *Die heilige Familie*, would only get him into greater trouble with his pietist family.

But Engels' reaction to the work (in his letter to Marx of 17 March) when a copy of *The Holy Family* finally reached him, was positive. He especially praised Marx's passages on the Jewish question, the history of Materialism, and Sue's *Mystères de Paris*, chapters which also contain parody. Nevertheless, Engels again criticised the length of the book, which appeared to him to be out of proportion to the importance of Bauer's journal. Moreover, Engels felt that the criticism of speculative philosophy would remain unclear to the larger public. Apart from this, Engels found that it was well written and comic: 'Sonst aber ist das ganze Buch prächtig geschrieben und zum Kranklachen.' But the functions of this humour and of the comic effect of the parody were not only aimed at the amusement of Marx's circle, but also at the destruction of Bauer's journal.

In the Preface of September 1844 Marx makes it clear that he understands Bauer's revision of speculative idealism to itself be speculative philosophy in caricature: thus one specific satiric function of parody and caricature in *The Holy Family* is the mirroring of Bauer's unwitting caricature of idealism in his revision of it in his 'critical criticism':

Was wir in der Bauerschen Kritik bekämpfen, ist eben die als Karikatur sich reproduzierende Spekulation.

(What we are fighting in Bauer's criticism, is speculative philosophy reproducing itself as caricature.)

Marx's statement that Bauer's method is a caricature of the philosophy it imitates or reproduces is put *a priori*, with little initial explanation. An implication of the particular formulation of Marx's argument given above is, however, that Bauer's combination of theology and critical philosophy does not only distort and caricature speculative idealism, but that it was in the nature of this speculative philosophy to reproduce itself as caricature. For if, as Marx argues, its presupposition that consciousness precedes man, as subject to object, is false, then the reproduction of itself is the reproduction of falsity. The distortion of Bauer's arguments by means of parody has thus the function of mirroring what must essentially happen in Bauer's reproduction of speculative philosophy.

One other specific function of parody in *The Holy Family* is the satiric imitation of the lack of clarity in the style of the *Literaturzeitung*. This is linked to an attack on the hypocrisy of the journal's claim that it is writing for the masses: Engel's opening chapter to their *Kritik der kritischen Kritik* begins:

> Die kritische Kritik, so erhaben sie sich über die Masse weiss, fühlt doch ein unendliches Erbarmen für dieselbe. Also hat die Kritik die Masse geliebt, dass sie ihren eingeborenen Sohn gesandt hat, auf dass alle, die an ihn glauben, nicht verloren werden, sondern das kritische Leben haben. Die Kritik wird Masse und wohnet unter uns und wir sehen ihre Herrlichkeit als die Herrlichkeit des eingebornen Sohnes vom Vater. D.h. die Kritik wird sozialistisch und spricht 'Von Schriften über den Pauperismus'. Sie sieht es nicht für einen Raub an, Gott gleich zu sein, sondern entäussert sich selbst, und nimmt Buchbindermeister-Gestalt an, und erniedrigt sich bis zum Unsinn, – ja zum kritischen Unsinn in fremden Sprachen . . .[5]

> (The critical criticism, no matter how elevated it feels itself to be above the masses, feels a limitless pity for them. So the criticism so loved the masses that it sent its (only) begotten son, so that all who believed in him would not be lost, but would have the critical life. The criticism became mass and dwells amongst us and we see its splendour as the splendour of the begotten son of the father. I.e. the criticism becomes socialistic and speaks 'Of Writings on Pauperism'. It does not regard it a crime to be equal with God, but incarnates itself and becomes a book-binder-master, and lowers itself to absurdity, – yes, to critical nonsense in strange tongues.)

Here Engels parodies Bauer's overuse of biblical language (in parody and otherwise) and alludes to Bauer's erstwhile role as theologian. One of the points made in the text of *The Holy Family* is that Bauer's apparent radical use of the Bible in the 1840s had concealed the theologian of old,[6] while his reading of the 'esoteric' Hegel had also concealed a conservative idealism.

One of the specific examples of biblical language used in Bauer's journal which is 'reproduced' in *The Holy Family* to demonstrate its lack of clarity of style is an attack by the Bauers on the biblical rhetoric and tone used in a 'conservative catechism', the *Katechismus für wahlberechtigte Bürger in Preußen*:

> Ein Katechismus mit gesalbter Salomonischer Sprache dessen Worte sanft wie eine Taube Zirb! Zirb! hinaufsteigen in die Region des Pathos und donnerähnlicher Aspekten.[7]

At the conclusion of *The Holy Family* this attack is turned around onto the *Literaturzeitung*: for it is the journal itself which, according to Marx, represents the 'dove-like' effect of the biblical rhetoric it had criticised in another. The dove-like effect of which the *Literaturzeitung* is accused is made all the more ironic by a reference to the 'lion-like' intention of the journal's satire on the dove-like conservatives. Marx's parody of the lines quoted from the *Literaturzeitung* occur in the final chapter, which is entitled 'Das kritische jüngste Gericht' ('The critical Last Judgement'):

> Und ich sah und hörete einen starken Engel, Herrn Hirzel, von Zürich aus mitten durch den Himmel fliegen.
> Und er hatte in seiner Hand ein Büchlein als wie das fünfte Heft der 'Allgemeinen Literaturzeitung'
> aufgetan; und er setzte seinen rechten Fuss auf die Masse und den linken auf Charlottenburg; und er schrie mit grosser Stimme, wie ein Löwe brüllt, und seine Worte erhoben sich wie eine Taube Zirb! Zirb! in die
> Region des Pathos und zu den donnerähnlichen Aspekten des kritischen jüngsten Gerichts.[8]

Herr Hirzel, the correspondent whose words were quoted previously and who is now shown repeating them in a caricature of the Last Judgement, is mocked as a dove in lion's clothing, as misusing the biblical rhetoric he had used in the 5th number of the journal, a part of which is then quoted by Marx.[9] Although a reading of that article reveals only one clearly biblical phrase, the apocalyptic 'und dieser Zeitpunkt ist nicht fern' ('and the time is not far off'), which predicts the final battle and victory of Bauer's criticism, Marx puts it into the context of a parody of the apocalypse, and juxtaposes it with Bauer's criticism of the *Katechismus für wahlberechtigte Bürger*. Bauer's *Allgemeine*

Literaturzeitung is also ironically substituted for the books of the
seven seals, from which are to be released the apocalyptic disasters
preceding the second coming of Christ and the parody of the journal
ends with the quotation of the 'Dies irae, dies illa', and the requiem
mass is intoned over the book which has been 'critically' judged and
condemned. The 'historical postscript' — in which 'not the world but
the critical literary journal' is described as having been destroyed —
ironically refers to Hirzel's warnings in the articles on Sue that the
world is in need of being saved[10] and turns the journal's judgement
on the world back onto itself then to relate unjustifiably the demise
of the journal to the criticism of it in *The Holy Family* itself. Here too
Marx and Engels also parody Szeliga's last article in the *ALZ* on
'Die Kritik', in which he speaks of criticism as the 'spirit of history',
and reminds his reader of the equation that 'Weltgeschichte ist
Weltgericht' — history is our judge. Equated with its targets in these
parodistic juxtapositions in *The Holy Family*, the *ALZ* is described
not only as having been judged by history, but as having been judged to
be as conservative as the targets it had once attacked. Here meta-
criticism is shown to have had itself as its subject with damning results.

The technique of substituting the journal for its target — the satirist
for an object of satire — which is used in *The Holy Family* would, on
the surface at least, appear to be similar to that used by Marx in the
Hegel. Epigramme to satirise Hegel's attack on Kant and Fichte. The
meta-critical nature of Marx's *Criticism of the Critical Critique* would
also appear to have a similar ironic mirroring character. One difference
is, however, that, while it could be shown that Marx's attack on Hegel
in 1837 might also be interpreted as a defence of Kant and Fichte,
Marx's attack on Bauer in 1844 is not always at the same time a
defence of Bauer's targets. Much of the *Holy Family* is concerned
primarily with attacking the presuppositions involved in Bauer's
judgements of issues and of his contemporaries. And often the parody
of 1845 attacks two targets at once — the critic Bauer as well as
Bauer's targets — freeing Marx from sympathy with either, and making
the parody satiric rather than ironic and reflective. If we were to agree
with Rüdiger Thomas[11] that Bauer was influenced by Fichte's
philosophy of self-consciousness, then we might also see his use ironic
parody as a device of self-reflection, which (as Schlegel believed of
irony) was to lead to increased self-consciousness. Primarily, however,
both Bauer's and Marx's use of parody in the 1840s was as a tool of
satire, and as a covert means of criticism. Yet parody still does not
appear to lead to a new terminology in *The Holy Family* and it is

only in the final chapter of *The German Ideology* (placed first by the MEGA editors) that a break with the style of Bauer is evident.

In both *The Holy Family* and *The German Ideology* a latent paradox exists in Marx's use of parody to attack Bauer's philosophy of the primacy of the self-conscious. For while irony and reflective parody conform to this philosophy they cannot conform to Marx's attack on such a philosophy, or to his argument for a method which will take as its object the 'real individual', without some change. In most cases, moreover, parody imitates and reflects arguments as they appear in literature, but comments on the world of the reader only obliquely. The 'crisis' of ridding *der reale Humanismus* of the terminology of speculative criticism is concealed in paradox in *The Holy Family*, in particular, in the use of the same methods of parody used by its target, speculative criticism. The surfacing of this crisis in *The German Ideology* foregrounds some of the more specific problems surrounding the use of parody as a critical method in 1844, such as the restriction of the audience to those familiar with the targets being attacked, and the redundancy suffered by the parody through the demise of its subject. Ironically a danger for all parodies successful in their task of 'destroying' their target, this applies not only to the collapse of Bauer's journal before the publication of *The Holy Family*, but, in the twentieth century, to the demise in popularity of the Bible. The almost paradoxical faith of the rationalist Marx in the immortality of the Bible, shown in the liberal quotation from it in the works of the 1840s, is echoed in the note from the editors of the first Moscow Institute edition of *The German Ideology* that quotations from the Bible would not be documented, as they were too numerous and, in any case, could be easily located or recognised by the reader.[12] The demise of the objects or sources of parody in Marx's works, such as Bauer's journal, limits the readership of them further as time progresses. The works of the 1840s and later years demonstrate an awareness of reader reaction in the broader context of the international community which contrasts with the Young Hegelian critiques of the early 1840s. And only when considered as a transitional method can parody be regarded as productive in these latter works. Yet one problem in determining the effect of parody on the style of the parodist is that we may run the danger of being answered in speculative manner.

There are few concrete signs of a connection between Marx's use of parody in the first sections of *The German Ideology* and the change to the direct and factual style of the chapter on Feuerbach:

the problem of giving a function to parody in *The German Ideology*, and to finding an explanation for Marx's attribution of a revolutionary character to some parody but not to others in the *Eighteenth Brumaire* remains to be discussed. Perhaps the most difficult element present in the discussion of the problem is the necessity of using a meta-language to describe the role of parody in effecting change in the terminology of Marx's works. Parody itself is a form of 'meta-literature', but in *The German Ideology* the issue of determining the role of parody in developing styles is complicated further by the fact that the literature and critical method being attacked and rejected by the parodist (in the works of the Young Hegelians) is parody itself.

Parody has at least two functions in *The German Ideology*: of attacking Bauer's overuse of parody and of freeing Marx from Bauer's 'critical criticism' and its methods, and from, that is, parody itself. In this sense Marx's use of parody in *The German Ideology* is problematical and symptomatic of a crisis in that work which may also be related to the so-called 'epistemological break' of 1845-6. Marx himself attributed a process of 'coming to terms with his past', and of 'understanding his self' to *The German Ideology*, and it is in this sense that we may understand his parodistic imitation of the Young Hegelians from whom he wished to break away. In that Marx's parody of Bauer's methods (and, that is, of parody itself) leads to the realisation that the transformation of his former models and their methods into targets of criticism was yet another way of chaining him to the past, it makes him aware of a dilemma, or crisis, which is solved by the rejection of that past as a subject for imitation or, even, criticism. In the sense that parody thereby negates and supersedes itself, it gains a final new role in Marx's work, which involves its own *Aufhebung* and rejection.

Notes

1. Louis Althusser, *For Marx* (transl. Ben Brewster), Middlesex, 1966, p. 35.
2. See MEGA 2, p. 87. See also David McLellan, *The Young Hegelians and Karl Marx*, p. 50.
3. See the open letters to the censor and the following article on the freedom of the journal to speak its criticism.
4. Mehring, *Aus dem literarischen Nachlass von Marx und Engels*, 3rd edn., vol. 2, Stuttgart, 1920.
5. MEGA 1/3, p. 180.
6. MEGA 1/3, p. 287.
7. Ibid., p. 181. And see, *Die allgemeine Literaturzeitung* (1843-4),

Charlottenburg, 2nd edn., 1847, Heft 6, p. 15.
8.   MEGA 1/3, p. 387.
9.   Ibid., p. 615. See also Bauer's *Allgemeine Literaturzeitung*, 1843-4, Charlottenburg, 2nd edn., 1847.
10.   See Chapter 8 of *Die heilige Familie, The Holy Family*.
11.   Rüdiger Thomas, *Der unbekannte junge Marx*, p. 205.
12.   MEGA 1/5, p. 642. The editors of the new MEGA have, however, decided to give references to the biblical quotations in Marx's works.

4 THE GERMAN IDEOLOGY: PARODY IN CRISIS

The German Ideology as edited by the Marx-Engels-Institute, Moscow, begins with the last and unfinished chapters on Feuerbach, in which Marx and Engels oppose their theory of historical Materialism to the philosophy of speculative idealism. In this context the earlier chapters of philosophical criticism against Bauer and Stirner — again made in part through biblical parody — reflect satirically the idealistic nature of Young Hegelian criticism, but also demonstrate the necessarily philosophical and literary nature of the earlier critical methods used by Marx and Engels themselves. For while the description of historical Materialism in the 1846 chapter on Feuerbach announces a method of dealing with the history of men and the material world produced by them, the chapters of 1845 (like *The Holy Family*) were still in part written about the linguistic and philosophical fallacies made in speculative criticism.

In his introduction to the first full edition of *The German Ideology* (left by Marx to the 'gnawing criticism of the mice'), Adoratskij wrote in 1933:

> . . . Das leider unvollendete, endgültig nicht ausgearbeitete Handschrift 'I. Feuerbach' enthält die erste systematische Darlegung ihrer historisch-philosophischen Auffassung der ökonomischen Entwicklungs-Geschichte der Menschen.[1]

Here Adoratskij calls the unfinished chapter on Feuerbach the 'first systematic exposition of their historical-philosophical concept of the economic development of man', and places it first in the newly edited manuscript, although it was the last chapter known to be written of the work, being composed between September 1845 and October 1846.[2] Thus, although *The German Ideology* may be designated as a work of the break, it must be kept in mind that this break occurs *within* the extant manuscript (never published by Marx in his lifetime) and not merely with it.

Adoratskij himself quotes Engels[3] as saying in his 1888 Introduction to *Ludwig Feuerbach und der Ausgang der klassischen deutschen Philosophie* (*Ludwig Feuerbach and the end of classical German philosophy*, referred to earlier), that the Feuerbach passage was not finished, and that the rest showed their development of the theory of historical materialism, but that the knowledge of economics expressed in it was still naive. According to Adoratskij, a plan worked out by Marx and Engels before the failed attempt at publication in July 1846 had placed the Feuerbach chapter second after the Preface of May/ August 1846, and before the earlier chapters on the Young Hegelians and the true socialists. In order not to see these chapters as a contradiction to the break evident in the chapter on Feuerbach and in the Preface (for they are similar in style to those of *The Holy Family*) the fact that they were written before the chapter on Feuerbach should not be ignored.

Read as stages on the road to the development of the new science of historical materialism, the early chapters cast a different light on the nature of the break, and on Althusser's argument against the 'supersession' of the past in the break, against, that is, the view that historical materialism was a development of, rather than a break with the past. The role of parody in these early chapters may also be given greater significance as one stage in a progression towards the new terminology when the actual chronology of the chapters is taken into account.

By any Aristotelian definition, the use of parody would be termed 'unscientific', so that Marx's avoidance of it after his break with the Young Hegelian school for the 'science' of historical materialism can be described as relegating it to what Althusser had called his 'prescientific' period. In, for example, his *Rhetorics*, Aristotle had distinguished the argumentation found in literature from that used in science, by claiming that literary argument proceeds dialectically (and intuitively), representing ideas but not analysing them, while science proceeds analytically (or demonstratively) and deductively from principles or axiomata to necessary knowledge. As, however, these axiomata may be given by intuitive knowledge, the argumentation of imaginative works may be granted as establishing new questions in science. The question of whether and how Marx's early works are *unscientific* (as Althusser tried to argue) must, in large part, be a question of terminology. What is interesting about Marx's use of parody in 1844-5 is to what extent and how it contributes to the break from the Young Hegelian school made and documented in those works and how it both relates to Marx's early use of literary parody and to his development of a new terminology in his 'mature' works.

The chapter on Feuerbach written for *The German Ideology* begins by making the point made in the Introduction of *The Holy Family*, that 'German criticism' had never left the realm of philosophy nor the idealism of Hegel. Now, however, Feuerbach too is included in the indictment, which is, moreover, made in terms which are much more direct and explicit than those used in *The Holy Family*. In *The German Ideology* Feuerbach is, for example, criticised as not having applied his 'realer Humanismus' to history:

> Soweit Feuerbach Materialist ist, kommt die Geschichte bei ihm nicht vor, und soweit er die Geschichte in Betracht zieht, ist er kein Materialist. Bei ihm fallen Materialismus und Geschichte ganz auseinander.

There may also be an oblique criticism of Marx and Engels' own method in earlier works to be read in the statement that the polemics of the Young Hegelians were incestuous.[4] Bauer's concept of self-consciousness and Stirner's *Der Einzige* are described as translations of Hegelian categories. The object of their criticism is, furthermore, rejected as being 'religious', and they are criticised for not having taken material reality as the subject matter of their criticism.[5] Instead of (as in *The Holy Family*) proceeding to a meta-criticism of the Hegelian *Kritik*, Marx and Engels now turn their attention to the material reality ignored by the *Kritik*: thus an awareness of a break in both their method and the objects of the method becomes clear. What follows is an analysis of the role played by the means of production in human history, an alternative analysis to Bauer's of the role of self-consciousness in human history.

Having 'worked through' their past in their parodistic imitation of Bauer's use of parody as a method of criticism, Marx and Engels thus wrote in their introduction to *The German Ideology* that language was 'inseparably linked to the material life of society and the labour process of men'.[6] Any philosophy, such as the critical criticism of Bauer, which ignored this connection, was in danger of directing attention to the wrong target. Hence, Marx accuses Bauer of fighting only against ideas, and him and other Young Hegelians of reducing this, moreover, to a battle against mere words. Marx wrote in the Introduction, which (like the chapter on Feuerbach) was completed after the parodistic chapters on Bauer and Stirner:

> . . . The most recent of them have found the correct expression for their activity when they declare they are only fighting against 'phrases'. They forget, however, that to these phrases they

themselves are only opposing other phrases and that they are in no
way combating the real existing words when they are merely
combating the phrases of this world . . .[7]

'Not criticism but revolution is the driving force of history', Marx
wrote a few pages later,[8] and it is clear that the condemnation of verbal
battles which we have here (and which is repeated in the *Eighteenth
Brumaire* of 1852) makes explicit Marx's own problem in *The Holy
Family* and in the earlier chapters of *The German Ideology*. In
articulating this problem and dissociating himself from it by transferring it back onto the Young Hegelians, Marx speaks directly, without
the use of parody or irony, and demonstrates his own release — made
within *The German Ideology* — from the fault he condemns. And not
only is the above made in direct language, but it is made in relationship
to an attempt to analyse the connection between language and the
material mode of production. Though this, as the introduction to the
Grundrisse of 1857 shows, also turned out to be a meta-linguistic
problem,[9] which Marx (and Marxist aestheticians after him) never
entirely resolved, its articulation as a problem in 1846 represents a step
out of their purely rhetorical parodistic attacks on the Young Hegelians
and the true socialist 'phrase-mongers'[10] of the earlier chapters. It was
in these chapters too that Marx had accused contemporaries like Karl
Grün of the sins of Marx's youth. Both had been members of the Bonn
Poet's Club, but now Marx turns against Grün for his use of *Sturm
und Drang* rhetoric,[11] ignoring the fact that the young Marx had also
used such weapons. In transferring these failings of his youth to his
adult contemporaries Marx had, however, remained within the area of
rhetorical criticism. Only when turning his attention to other material
issues and to arguing that languages too could not be understood apart
from these issues, did Marx finally release himself from the traditional
weaponry of those whom he was attacking. While the Introduction
and chapter on Feuerbach introduce new material and the basis for a
new method of analysis, the material dialectic, the chapters on Bauer
and Stirner are entrenched in the 'meta-criticism' characteristic of
The Holy Family, and remain trapped by the categories and terminology which they criticise.

Parody in those chapters restricts Marx and Engels to the vocabulary
and method of their arguments, not only because parody was a tool
used by Bauer, but because in the structure of the literary parody the
object of satire is reproduced (through quotation or imitation) before
it is attacked or refunctioned, and thus contributes textual material to

the parody, which may appear to limit its scope. Yet parody in world literature had often been used to refunction and change literary traditions into something new, to create a literary work from the destruction of old literary traditions, and it was in this sense too that Kant appeared to understand the function of parody and wit. And for Hegelians, Cervantes' *Don Quixote* could be taken as a paradigm for a type of innovative or 'dialectical' parody, in which the target of satire (the knightly romance) is quoted to form the basis of the parodistic work before being *aufgehoben*, or superseded by the parody. In the case of *Don Quixote* literary historians have tried to argue for this dialectical process in suggesting that from its parody of the romance *Don Quixote* had given birth to the modern novel. This perspective is one also used by Marx in the *Eighteenth Brumaire* to decide which parodies in history have been accompanied by change and which not, and in this he could, in general terms, be said to be adhering still to both Kant's and Hegel's concepts of parody.

Parody in *Don Quixote* can be called open, and characteristic of new challenges to established authority. In his preface to *Don Quixote* Cervantes himself had mocked the blind use of literary authorities and explicitly related his use of parody to this anti-authoritative attitude. Marx's use of authorities in his poetry, drama and novel fragments of 1837 could not be described as parodistic in this open or dialectical sense. Rather, the dependent use of authorities was ambivalently joined to a type of reflective 'closed' parody. But although *The Holy Family* used parody satirically against Bauer, while also attacking the closed nature of the Hegelians' system, it too could not extricate Marx and Engels from the method of the system they had recently been defending. Parody had necessarily to free Marx from the terminology of the Young Hegelians and his own previous works, and from parody itself. Ironically parody used to mirror Bauer's use of parody had created a new 'closed' system from which Marx had to escape after 'escaping' from the Young Hegelians. Parody had eventually to be exchanged for another method: the awareness of the nature of this crisis marks the beginning of its solution.

For Thomas Kuhn, author of *The Structure of Scientific Revolutions,* the demarcation of scientific discovery revealed similar moments of crisis preceding revolutionary change. Kuhn's account of scientific revolutions may, over all, be seen as being plagued by the difficulty of establishing a theory on the basis of the relative sociological evidence he uses, yet the concept of crisis bears further explanation. In broad terms an analogy may be drawn between the role of parody in *The*

German Ideology and the role of crisis in the history of scientific discovery outlined by Kuhn, as the history of the exchange of one paradigm for another. This pattern may be derived from the types of methods of criticism used in the text of *The German Ideology*, consisting as it does of the new theory of historical materialism and the Young Hegelian method which it attacks. The analogy with Kuhn's theory cannot be extended very far, however, in that Kuhn is dealing with the rejection of paradigms by societies while in *The German Ideology* this rejection and the crisis which surrounds it appear to belong to the writers alone, though it could also be argued that their break with the language and theory of the Young Hegelian school was also a break with the conditions maintaining that philosophy and style. What is interesting about the role of parody in this 'exchange of paradigms' is that its use is what helps to provoke the crisis preceding Marx's 'liberation' from the terminology of the Young Hegelians. It might even be said that an 'epistemological crisis' in *The German Ideology* is evident in the attempts of the author to free himself from the terminology and methods of the Young Hegelians. If it cannot be shown that parody assists Marx in changing the terminology and methods it has (by imitation) helped to restrict him to, it is obvious that it contributes to the crisis which precedes the change evident in the chapter on Feuerbach. And in the sense that parody can be said to contribute to the crisis preceding change in the terminology of *The German Ideology* it can be described as a means to the supersession of the Young Hegelian style in Marx's work. While parody in Marx's work had formerly represented both the object of criticism (for example, Bauer's use of biblical parody) and the means of its criticism, it now appears to have been made part of a broader dialectical method leading to change and, ironically, to its own supersession. Marx's own evaluation of some parody as dialectical will be the subject of the analysis of his *Eighteenth Brumaire* of 1852.

The break which is made in *The German Ideology* follows on Marx's development from Kant in 1837 through the Right and Left Hegelians to Feuerbach. Subjects from these earlier works reappear in 1845-6 and in the chapter on Feuerbach receive analysis. Yet a comparison of the parodistic treatment of the first chapter of the Gospel of John in *The German Ideology* with its parody from the mouth of Grethe in *Scorpion und Felix* will illustrate both the contrast between the chapter on Feuerbach and the parodistic style of the critiques of Bauer and Stirner in *The German Ideology* and the contrast between the use of parody in 1844-5 and that of 1837. In 54a (51a) 3 of *The German*

Ideology,[12] entitled 'Offenbarung Johannis des Theologen oder "Die Logik der neuen Weisheit" ' Stirner's *Der Einzige und sein Eigentum* is mockingly described as the new Messiah of the age, as Bauer's journal had been in *The Holy Family*:

> Im Anfang war das Wort, der Logos. In ihm war das Leben, und das Leben war das Licht der Menschen. Und das Licht scheinet in die Finsternis und die Finsternis haben es nicht begriffen. Das war das wahrhaftige Licht, es war in der Welt, und die Welt kannte es nicht. Es kam in sein Eigentum und die Seinen nahmen ihn nicht auf. Wie viele ihn aber aufnahmen, denen gab er Macht Eigentümer zu werden, die an [den N] amen des Einzigen glauben. [Aber we] r hat den Einzigen je ge [sehen?]

> (In the beginning was the Word. In Hîm was life; and the life was the light of men. And the light shineth in darkness; and the darkness comprehended it not. That was the true light, it was in the world and the world knew it not. It came into its own, and its own received him not. But to those who did receive him, to them he gave the power to become property-owners [to 'come into their own'], who believe in the name of the unique one [the ego of Stirner's *Der Einzige und sein Eigentum*: *The Ego and his Own*]. But who has ever seen the unique one?)

Marx's parody of the biblical passage consists in the extension of a pun on the title of Stirner's book, *Der Einzige und sein Eigentum*. The incarnation of God is ironically replaced by the incarnation of *der Einzige*, the individual ego in his private property, and the cult of private property ownership equated with an irrational belief in the sacred nature of the individual ego which has 'never been seen'. The idealistic role given the ego and private property by Stirner is mocked by the analogy with an agnostic description of the incarnation of God in matter in John I and also, by implication, given the role of both a blasphemy and a heresy against the Bible, in that the incarnation of the Spirit in matter was not, as the 'incarnation' of the ego in private property, to be of a permanent kind. Hegel's philosophy, as the 'Bible' of the Young Hegelians and as a theodicy of history, is also ironised.

In *Der Einzige und sein Eigentum* (which had appeared just prior to *The Holy Family* in 1844), Stirner had maintained that Feuerbach's attitude to man was basically theological in giving divinity to the human thinker. Stirner's concept of the individual was, according to

Stirner, to be free of this. But Marx has ironically raised Stirner's individual to the position of a pseudo-Messiah in an argument *ad hominem* in substituting *der Einzige* for Christ in his parody of John I. Stirner is thus both condemned for 'mystifying' property and for doing what he had accused Feuerbach of having done. Although Marx again turns an argument made by his target back onto that target itself, it is not in explicit defence of the target's object of satire (here Feuerbach) as it was in 1837 in the case, for example, of the satires of Hegel's attacks on Kant. It is (as the parody used in *The Holy Family*) satiric, in contrast to the reflective irony of 1837.

Yet the specific satirical functions of parody in *The German Ideology* are often lost in the extension of the parody throughout the whole of a section in the chapter. The chapter on Stirner, for example, (written September 1845 to May 1846) entitled 'Saint Max', is written after the form of the Bible, beginning:[13] 'Altes Testament: Der Mensch', '1. Genesis, d.i. ein Menschenleben', before proceeding to the discussion of 'Saint Max'. It includes, moreover,[14] a type of *had gadya*[15] poem in which the image of the avenging angel slaughtering all other slaughterers is replaced by that of Marx's *Criticism of the Critical Critique*. There appears to be an element of self-irony in the depiction of Marx's essentially Young Hegelian form of meta-criticism as the slaughtering of the slaughterers. Marx's indication of the similarity between himself and his targets appears also to point to his dilemma of finding a new method and terminology from within an attack on old subjects. Basically the biblical parody used in these chapters juxtaposes the philosophy of Bauer and Stirner with the Bible to mirror the theological nature of the Young Hegelian Kritik, but its point is made repetitively. Another example is to be found in Marx's parody of the Apocalypse (Chapter 17, verses 3, 5 and 6) in his criticism of Stirner:

> Der Apokalyptiker hat diesmal nicht genau geweissagt. Jetzt endlich, nachdem Stirner den Mann proklamiert hat, kann man es aussprechen, dass er so hätte sagen müssen: Und er brachte Mich in die Wüste des Geistes. Und ich sahe den Mann sitzen auf einem rosinfarbenen Tier, das war voll Lästerung der Namen — und an seiner *Stirn* geschrieben den Namen, das Geheimnis, *den Einzigen* — und ich sahe den Mann trinken von dem Blute des Heiligen etc.
> Wir geraten also jetzt in die Wüste des *Geistes*.[16]

Marx begins by ironically claiming credibility for his new version of the Apocalypse by maintaining that the old apostle did not prophesy correctly 'this time'. The biblical prophecy is also shown to have been contradicted by Stirner, in that he has prophesied the new age as that of *Der Einzige und sein Eigentum*. Stirner's contradiction is turned into the parody of the Apocalypse we have here: the beast of the Apocalypse bears on his forehead (*Stirn* meaning forehead as well as suggesting a pun on Stirner) the 'secret' of his book on the individual and private property. The mysterious and mystified character given property in Stirner's work had also been attacked as an aspect of Proudhon's theory in *The Holy Family*.[17] But Stirner's secret is described not as the 'key to heaven' but as the entrance into the 'desert of the Spirit', a reference to the barrenness of Stirner's spiritualism. The reader of *The German Ideology* was apparently expected to know the writings of Bauer and Stirner which are often only partially alluded to or described. While much literary parody has also served to make its model memorable, some parody has had the prime function of bringing about its demise, through canonising it in a new and usually distorted form in its text. Thus, if Stirner and Bauer were only to be known from Marx's parody of them, it would be a distorted version of their writings which would be known.

Marx has often been accused of misquoting the arguments he was attacking in works which did not use parody as a method of criticism. This misquotation of texts in the parodies — to produce laughter as well as a critical attitude in the reader — exaggerated this tendency. It is this aspect of parody, as the distorted quotation of texts, which makes its use suspicious as a tool of criticism in *The German Ideology*: for, in that it works by allusion and partial quotation, it does not provide an accurate method of analysing texts. Parody is also dependent on the reader's knowledge of the texts parodied, as well as on his powers of association (as, for example, on the ability to associate Hegel's *Phenomenology* as the 'Bible' of the Young Hegelians with the use of biblical parody, or even *Stirn* with *Stirner*, etc.). Parody may be both an indefinite method of criticism and a short-lived one when the public conversant with the texts being parodied disappears with those texts. The disappearance of the objects of its satire, the texts successfully made redundant by the parodist, may (as argued earlier) contribute to the redundancy of the parody itself. Numerous references to *Don Quixote* in *The German Ideology* (largely to satirise the Young Hegelians as spectre-fighters in their idealist critique) betray a continuing admiration for that book, yet while it might be said that the use of literary parody in *The Holy Family* was at least appropriate to attacking Bauer's literary journal, its use in *The German Ideology* to attack the combination of theology and fiction in speculative philosophy produces the paradox which makes parody symptomatic of a crisis in that work. One aspect of this crisis was, as we have argued, the use of parody as both a tool of satire against the Hegelians and as a way of reflecting and mockingly imitating their own over-use of parody. But yet another contradiction which arose in *The German Ideology* was between development of a 'scientific' theory of historical materialism and the continued use of parody, a method of criticism concerned with literary rather than material objects and with reflecting the process of literary discussion rather than with the presentation of reality.

After 1846 less use is made of parody by Marx and Engels, but in 1852 the roles of deliberate and unwitting parody in historical change are explicitly connected with both crisis and revolution in the *Eighteenth Brumaire*. The 'silent' role of parody in these processes of change in *The German Ideology* is thus made explicit in 1852. Again, as with Marx's 1841 condemnation of the censor silently 'alluded to' in his poetry of 1837, a later work describes the process silently at work in earlier texts.

Notes

1.   MEGA 1/5, x.
2.   Ibid., p. 8.
3.   MEGA 1/5, XI.
4.   MEGA 1/5, p. 5, 'Ihre Polemik gegen Hegel und gegen einander . . .'
5.   Ibid., p. 1.
6.   Marx and Engels, *The German Ideology*, Moscow, 1968, p. 16.
7.   Ibid., p. 30 ff.
8.   Ibid., p. 50.
9.   Here Marx appears to leave himself open to the charge that his own comment is thereby also linked to external factors which he should have given but has not. Yet Marx's statement does nevertheless set language into the historical-social context which will provide the information missing from the meta-linguistic statement and which makes the verification of speech-acts from external evidence possible. Marx's rejection of purely meta-linguistic modes of analysis such as parody may hence also be seen to have played a part in his development of a materialist view of language.
10.   *The German Ideology*, p. 529.
11.   Ibid., p. 635.
12.   MEGA 1/5, p. 249.
13.   MEGA 1/5, p. 100.
14.   Ibid., pp. 114-16.
15.   The *Had Gadya* of the Passover *seder* has a similar form to that of

The House that Jack Built or the French, *Jacques le bonhomme.*

16.   MEGA 1/5, p. 128.
17.   MEGA 1/3, p. 212 f.

5 THE EIGHTEENTH BRUMAIRE: HISTORY AS PARODY

The lesson learnt in 1846 was that when the object to be changed by parody was parody itself then both method and object had to be refunctioned. The lesson taught about parody as it appears in history in the *Eighteenth Brumaire of Louis Napoleon* is, similarly, that the parodistic imitation of historical periods has only accompanied change when transitional, when used as a means to criticism. Hegel's description of parody as a means of returning to the past to criticise it will be recalled. Having freed his own style of the limitations of parody by 1848 (when much of the literature of the German *Vormärz* was still producing examples of the method), Marx condemned in the *Eighteenth Brumaire* and *Die grossen Männer des Exils* of 1852 the unwitting parody of past historical periods and past literary movements which had produced no innovations. And here Kant's description of parody as innovative is echoed. In their condemnation of Romanticism as an outdated style still being used by their contemporaries, the exiles of the 1848 Revolution, in *Die grossen Männer des Exils*, Marx and Engels also indicate why they now wish to suppress knowledge of their own youthful imitation of the Romantics and another reason for what we have termed the 'second censorship' of Marx's poetry.

Die grossen Männer des Exils, written shortly after the completion of the *Eighteenth Brumaire* in May and June 1852, was not published by Marx and Engels, and was, according to the editor of the Dietz Ausgabe, partly written in Dronke's hand (that is, Part I, pp. 235-53 of MEWA, volume 8), while the rest was in Engels' writing, with additions by Marx. As was the case with Engels' attack on the literary true socialists (written after *The German Ideology*) *Die grossen Männer des Exils* ostensibly attacked liberal writers who represented a failed cause, in this case the failure of the 1848 Revolution. *Die grossen Männer* opens with a motto taken from Klopstock's *Messias*, imitated by Marx in 1836-7 and parodied by Engels in his *Triumph* of 1842:

'Singe, unsterbliche Seele,
der sündigen Menschen Erlösung' —
durch Gottfried Kinkel.

(Sing, immortal soul,
of the redemption of sinful mankind' –
   through Gottfried Kinkel.)

The verses precede, ironically, an attack on this Messiah, Gottfried
Kinkel, which is made in the form of a biography. Kinkel's youthful
identification with Novalis' *Heinrich von Ofterdingen* is mocked as
being a travesty of that work, just as Louis Napoleon's declaration of
himself as Emperor in December 1851 is satirised as a bad parody of
his namesake's *Eighteenth Brumaire* in the work of that name written
a few months earlier. What is forgotten, or concealed, by Marx and
Engels in their attack on Kinkel's youthful Romanticism is, of
course, their own. There is, in the terms of the historical developments leading to 1851 (apart from their desire to break from that
idealist part of their youth), good reason for this, in view, for example,
of the emergence of a revival of Romanticism in both literature and
politics in the reign of Friedrich Wilhelm IV of Prussia. Friedrich
Wilhelm's support for the Catholic Church – in the rebuilding of the
Cologne Cathedral, and in the display of the Holy Cloak in Trier in
1844 (attacked by Marx in the conclusion of the *Eighteenth Brumaire*
to connect, perhaps, the retrograde events following 1848 in France
with the similar failure of the Revolution in Germany) – had brought
Romanticism back into politics. Robert Blum, an editor of *Vorwärts*,
and radical member of the 1848 Frankfurt Parliament, who was
executed by the counter-revolutionaries in 1849, had also led an attack
on the ultra-Montanism of Friedrich Wilhelm IV.

   In 1852 Marx was in the first year of his permanent exile, having
left Germany and, it must be remembered, his youthful verse behind
him. This physical break with his past, with, that is, his Romantic
verse of 1837 as well as with the Romanticism of Friedrich Wilhelm
IV's Prussia, appears to be reflected in the vehement attack on
Romantic elements in Kinkel's past, which are described as being still
alive in Kinkel's present. The condemnation of Kinkel's unimaginative
imitation of false Romantic sentiment also appears to describe, either
unintentionally or ironically, the juvenilia left behind in Cologne in
1851: '. . . Die erlogene Romantik, die Travestie und Karikierung alter
Historien und Abeteuer, welche Gottfried aus Mangel an eigenem
Fonds anderen nacherlebt'.[1] The 1852 criticisms contain not only
condemnation of unproductive parody but of the imitation of
Romantic authors, indicating a new stage in Marx's writing and a break
between the juvenilia and the mature works which will not be repaired.

One indication of this new stage is the use made by Marx and Engels of their own past as an image of the anachronisms of the present. Thus Marx condemns the Romantic verse of the 1840s as ultra-conservative as well as plagiaristic[2] from within his new position in the theory of historical materialism. Despite the return to literary criticism (and to parody and metaphor) in this unpublished work of 1852, like the *Eighteenth Brumaire*, it is also a commentary on the politics of reaction. Moreover, it represents another revision of Marx's and Engels' attitude to the *Tendenzdichter* of the *Vormärz* condemned by Heine in his satire *Atta Troll* of 1842. Heine's satire is for example used in *Die grossen Männer* to equate Ruge with the bumbling *Tendenzbär* Atta Troll: Ruge is seen as having become, like other Young Hegelians and liberals of 1848, a mixture of the reactionary and the revolutionary for Marx and Engels.[3] Here and elsewhere in *Die grossen Männer* a technique is used to condemn the uncritical, farcical imitation of past periods which is not unlike the literary parody used by Marx and Engels in earlier writings. Yet parody is described in the works of 1852 as only a stage in the development of old forms and of old models into new images: it is both dialectical in this sense and combined with a form of direct criticism which places less emphasis on the literary images and expressions which had filled the earlier works.

In *Scorpion und Felix*, the fragment of a novel of 1833, Marx had described history as the repetition of the sublime by the absurd, as Heine had earlier in his *Ideen. Das Buch le Grand* of 1824. In *Scorpion und Felix*[4] Hegel had been described as a dwarf following the great philosopher Kant, as other great figures of history had been followed by lesser men. No mention is made of Hegel's own concept of history in the novel, and Marx develops his theory of history in the context of a mocking application of the philosophy of David Hume and his idea of later developments replacing earlier ones to the detriment of greatness:

> As soon as the first disappears the last begin to take their place at table and vigorously stretch out their legs.

In the early work dwarves replace giants and philistines genii, in a similar manner to Heine's Hegelian view of history as a series of repetitions, except that here Hegel too is counted by Marx amongst the dwarves!

In *Scorpion und Felix* Marx had tried to imitate the 'genial' irony and parody of authors such as Laurence Sterne and Heine. But he had

also used parody self-consciously as a metaphor for historical decline
and for his own epigonal writing. In 1852, however, parody has come
to be seen as a transitional means to the liberation of a new generation
from the language and models of the past. Hegel's description of
parody as the means by which an age returns to its past in order to
criticise it is taken by Marx as an imperative – not only in the sense
that retrograde imitations of the past in history are condemned, but
also in the sense that parody as an end in itself is rejected. Marx's
The Eighteenth Brumaire of Louis Napoleon begins:

> Hegel bemerkt irgendwo, dass alle grossen weltgeschichtlichen
> Tatsachen und Personen sich sozusagen zweimal ereignen. Er hat
> vergessen hunzuzufügen: das eine Mal als Tragödie, das andere Mal
> als Farce.[5]

> (Hegel remarks somewhere that all great world-historical events
> and personages occur so to speak twice. He has forgotten to add:
> the first time as tragedy, the other time as farce.)

Marx appears to have borrowed the idea of describing Napoleon III's
coup as a parodistic repetition of Napoleon I's eighteenth brumaire
from a letter by Engels of 3 December 1851. But Marx is also mocking
Hegel. 'Somewhere' in Hegel was, of course, his *Philosophy of History*,
condemned by Marx in *The German Ideology*[6] as the last expression
of idealism in the analysis of history. The parodistic quotation of
Hegel, which ironically assumes that the readers most hurt by the
casualness of the reference will be those Hegelians who already know it,
also assumes to pre-empt the oblivion awaiting Hegel's philosophy of
history which is to follow Marx's analysis, in that it gives no exact
reference for the quote. An example of parody used in its negative
sense as a metaphor for history seen as farce follows in Marx's analysis
of the 1848 Revolution as an uncritical and unproductive parody of
the bourgeois Revolution of 1789. Marx thus establishes two ways in
which he will use the word parody: as a critical means to change (in this
case to supersede the idealist philosophy of history), and as a metaphor
through which to satirise the uncritical imitation of past historical
periods. The first method, together with its idea of a dialectical form
of parody, also replaces the imitative and reflective forms of parody
found earlier in Marx's work. While critical parody can serve the present,
imitative parody (as found in literature or history) is rejected as serving
only the past.

To Marx the imitation made by the 1789 Revolutionaries of the Roman Republicans had only been a stage in their initiation of a new Revolution and could, therefore, be historically justified. For the revolution of 1848, however, the imitation of the bourgeois Revolution of 1789 had become an end, rather than a means to change and, as a consequence, their imitation a type of farce, and an example of parody in its second, negative sense.[7] In the *Eighteenth Brumaire* Marx argued for the necessity of a proletarian revolution, and applied a dialectic to the history of nineteenth-century revolutions, to describe how a period of history could make a previous age a part of itself before making an end of it. It is this concept of material history which parodies Hegel's history of the idea, and which was also to replace it. Marx must have known very well the passage in Hegel which he describes vaguely as 'somewhere' in Hegel's work when writing the introductory sentence of the *Eighteenth Brumaire*. Not only does the essay refunction Hegel, but the letter from Engels to Marx of 3 December 1851 (from which Marx borrows the idea of the eighteenth brumaire as farce) mentions the relevant passage on the repetition of history from the third part of the *Philosophy of History*. Ironically, the Hegelian dialectic of the conservation and cessation of the thesis in its *Aufhebung*, is made to fit Marx's own treatment of Hegel's philosophy of history, his application of the dialectic to material history, and the description of the Jacobins' acquisition and renunciation of the masks of another age in the Revolution of 1789 as a way to revolutionary change.

Christian Dietrich Grabbe's dramatic comedy, *Scherz, Satire, Ironie und tiefere Bedeutung*, written in 1822 and first published in 1827, had taken Metternich's Restoration as its scene of action. Into the Restoration Grabbe had put the devil in the guise of a cleric, making it into a hell on earth, and the Church the cause of this hell. The devil is also used by Grabbe to parody the concept of history as a world theatre and to turn that *topos* into the idea that repetitive history can — like theatre — become farce. This is done when the devil is made into the author of the French Revolution:

Übrigens habe ich schon mehrere Werke ans Licht gestellt, wie erst kürzlich die Französische Revolution, ein Trauerspiel in vierzehn Jahren, mit einem Prologe von Ludwig XV.[8]

(Moreover, I have already brought many works into the light of day, such as, only recently, the French Revolution, a tragedy in fourteen years, with a Prologue by Louis XV.)

Yet the devil laments that the piece was badly received, and 'guillotined' by the critics. The topos of the world stage, the *theatrum mundi*,
transposed by Hegel onto history, is extended by Grabbe: if history
occurs on a world stage, then each event in history may be termed a
play. But if these plays are also part of a diachronic development then
the one can be seen to be a development of the other – and the minor
a parody of the major:

> Jetzt beschäftige ich mich mit einem Possenspiele, welches unter
> dem Titel: der griechische Freiheitskampf vom Verfasser der
> Französischen Revolution, im Verlage des türkischen Kaisers
> erscheint.

Alexander Pope is also said to have asked of Cromwell, 'Pray do me the
favour, Sir, to inform me: is this your Tragedy or your Comedy?'[9]
After failing to have his tragedy (the French Revolution) repeated a
second time (after its first night) either in Prussia, Austria or England
due to the 'severity of censorship', the devil has turned his talents into
the writing of a 'small farce', the Greek wars of liberation, to appear in
the 'publishing house' of the Turkish Emperor. Grabbe's irony is
ambivalent: is the farce to be seen as a poor imitation of the French
Revolution, or as an attempt to escape the censor? Why does it appear
in the environs of the Turkish Empire? – because it is to be seen as
an attempt to overthrow it, or as complying with the demands of the
censor? The censor had often been compared to the executioner and
the thoughts of those censored by him often referred to as having been
'guillotined'. Here Grabbe reverses the image and compares the
(conservative) executioners of the French Revolution to the censor,
ironically to describe history in a play to be written, produced and
perhaps banned like any other piece of writing. Grabbe's use of
ambiguous irony is itself a comment on the restrictions placed on the
playwright by the Restoration censorship in Germany, which was
strengthened after the *Karlsbader Beschlüsse* of 1819. But it is
'double-edged' as well as ambiguous in that it clearly mocks both kinds
of censorship, the literary and the historical.

Marx's treatment of history as a succession of tragedy and farce,
made in the *Eighteenth Brumaire* in 1852, is similar to Grabbe's
description of 1789 as tragedy followed by smaller farcical revolutions.
Yet Marx was not just drawing a metaphor from Hegel for a fictional

play within a play as was Grabbe, but proving Hegel's view of history wrong on the basis of material history itself, as well as offering a criticism of the imitative nature of the bourgeois Revolution of 1848. In the *Eighteenth Brumaire* it is Hegel's philosophy of history which is 'turned onto its head', together with all metaphorical and ideal concepts of history. Grabbe and Heine had only made Hegel's metaphor of history as a series of events on the world stage dynamic by turning it into a metaphor for the parodistic repetition by itself of human history. In 1824, in *Ideen. Das Buch le Grand*, Heine had described the Restoration as a comic parody of the *ancien régime*, seeing the 'fat Bourbons' waddling back onto the stage of world history in unwitting parody of France's pre-revolutionary age. Even the young Engels appears to have been influenced by Heine's interpretation of history when he was writing (under the pseudonym of Friedrich Oswald) his essay 'Retrograde Zeichen der Zeit'.[10] The essay speaks, as had Heine in his essay of 1833, 'Verschiedenartige Geschichtsauffassung', of the static nature of theories of recurrence in nature and history:

> Nichts Neues unter der Sonne! Das ist eine jener glücklichen Pseudowahrheiten, denen die brillanteste Karriere zugedacht war, die von Mund zu Mund ihren Triumphzug um die Erde machten und nach Jahrhunderten noch so oft zitiert werden, als kämen sie erst eben zur Welt. Die echten Wahrheiten sind selten so glücklich gewesen . . .

> (Nothing new under the sun! That is one of these happy pseudo-truths, which are promised a brilliant career, which make their triumphant way around the earth, and are quoted just as often after centuries of use, as if they had only just arrived in the world. Genuine truths have rarely been so lucky . . .)

One of the objects of Ruge's attack on romanticism in the *Halle Yearbooks* of 1840[11] was the same historical school of law attacked by Heine in his essay 'Verschiedenartige Geschichtsauffassung'. One of its slogans, attacked by Heine, as well as by Engels in the passage just quoted, was Solomon's proverb 1, 9, that there was 'nothing new under th sun'. Heine had remarked ironically that there was even nothing new in this slogan of the historical school, as it had been taken from Solomon, and that it expressed the same indifference to politics typical of the Goethean 'Kunstperiode'. Heine contrasted the Hegelian philosophy of history with that of the historical school, describing the former as the description of the unfolding of reason in a future golden age of freedom. But Heine chose to align himself neither with the past (as represented by the views of the historical school) nor with the futurologists of the Hegelian school, but with the present and the immediate social needs of man. In his final sentence Heine affirmed his faith in the social revolution, and in a different slogan from that of the historical school, in, that is, the words of St Just, 'Le pain est le droit du peuple'.

Heine had used Solomon's proverb, that 'nothing under the sun is new' to satirise the circular nature of the concept of history as offered by the historical school of Ranke and to oppose it with the Hegelian view of history as progress, just as he opposed unconscious parody, with critical, dialectical parody in history. Engels both names Heine in a following passage of his essay on history and applies Heine's image of history as a sequence of tragedy and farce to the Restoration:

> . . . Unsere Salons sind schon geschmückt, Stühle, Tische, Schränke und Sofas im style de la Renaissance, und es fehlt nur noch, dass man Heinen eine Perücke aufsetzte und Bettinen in einen Reifrock presste, um das siècle vollständig wiederherzustellen.[12]

In the *Französische Zustände* of 1832 Heine had named the Carlists, the party of the then deposed Bourbons, together with the republican opposition (who with them made up the opposition to the July Monarchy) as 'plagiarists of the past'. Both, Heine argued, showed a lack of political imagination in using slogans and ideas of the past: for the Carlists these slogans were the clichés of the *ancien régime*, while for the republican *amis du peuple* slogans were the revived battle cries of 1793. In his article of 3 October 1840, published in *Lutezia*, Heine explained this point in greater detail, maintaining it was still true for 1840. For Heine the contemporaneous revolutionary movement in France was to a great extent identical with the bourgeois revolutions of 1789 and 1830. The next step in history had to be a progressive one towards the 'permanent' social revolution.

Heine was not concerned with transforming the bourgeois Revolution of 1789 into a proletarian victory in 1840 but with ensuring the victory of the 'sensualistic' Dantonist revolution over the Robespierrian Terror. It is here that Heine and Marx part ways in their respective works of 1840 and 1852. Nevertheless, it cannot be denied that both saw the revolutions of the nineteenth century as parodying that of 1789, and the course of the bourgeois revolution in the new century

as consequently undialectical, as an alternation of apparent oppositions
which led back to each other, but never to anything new. Later the
bourgeois world is shown in Heine's poems of the *Romanzero* of
1852, as in *Weltlauf*'s analysis of the haves and the have-nots of the
world in terms of those inside the wheel of fortune and those outside
it who can never climb on, as having developed a new closed society
in which change had become repetitious. There Heine's own use of
parody is dialectical: *Weltlauf* both parodies conflicting stories in the
Bible, which defend the beggar Lazarus, but also the capitalist in the
parable of the talents and the glorification of *Haben* − the having
attacked by Marx and Engels in Stirner's analysis of private property
in *The German Ideology*.[13]

Both Heine and Marx use parody to create new from old texts
in a dialectical manner while using the word parody in its second
negative sense to describe the unintentional imitation of historical
periods in history.[14] The second paragraph of the *Eighteenth Brumaire*
introduces this analysis into the analysis of history as parodistic
repetition:

> Men make their own history, but they do not make it just as they
> please; they do not make it under circumstances chosen by them-
> selves, but under circumstances directly encountered, given, and
> transmitted from the past. The tradition of all the dead generations
> weighs like a nightmare on the brain of the living. And just when the
> they seem engaged in revolutionising themselves and things, in
> creating something that has never yet existed, precisely in such
> periods of revolutionary crisis they anxiously conjure up the spirits
> of the past to their service and borrow from them names, battle
> cries, and costumes in order to present the new scene of world
> history in this time-honoured disguise and this borrowed language.
> Thus Luther donned the mask of the apostle Paul, the Revolution
> of 1789 to 1814 draped itself alternately as the Roman Republic
> and the Roman Empire, and the Revolution of 1848 knew nothing
> better to do than to parody, now 1789, now the revolutionary
> tradition of 1793 to 1795. In like manner a beginner who has
> learned a new language always translates it back into his mother
> tongue, but he has assimilated the spirit of the new language and
> can freely express himself in it only when he finds his way in it
> without recalling the old and forgets his native tongue in the use of
> the new.[15]

In this passage Marx has set out to describe the problem besetting all innovators, of freeing themselves from their past. The problem of invention had obsessed Marx in works of 1837, such as the poem *Schöpfung*. But, as we have seen, the poet had had eventually to take recourse to imitating the works of the *Sturm und Drang* and Romantic genii, failing his own success at 'inventing' verse. Marx's ambivalent attitude to his authorities in these works provided no real possibility of breaking with them. The difficulty of 'breaking with the past' has also been seen to have been a problem for Marx in the 1840s where he had used parody in imitation of his targets of satire, the old authorities of his Young Hegelian period. The dilemma resulting from this experience of using parody as a means to imitation rather than innovation was described in an earlier section of the study as the 'crisis' which preceded the change to a more direct method of criticism in *The German Ideology* in 1846. With that the late eighteenth century's favoured methods of poetry and wit are dropped for more effective methods of analysis.

Marx's 1869 Preface to the second edition of the *Eighteenth Brumaire* of 1852 had criticised, but nevertheless singled out, Hugo's satirical *Napoleon le Petit* from other reactions to Napoleon III's 'coup' of 1851. Hugo had followed, as Marx points out, a tradition of satirising the Napoleon legend popular since 1815. This tradition had, however, remained 'largely unnoticed outside of France'. Marx's recognition of the *coterie* nature of audiences for satire and parody is accompanied, as reflected in his criticism of the limitations of Hugo's satire as political comment, by criticism of the limitations of the literary word *per se* as a form of criticism. The moment of 'revolutionary crisis' is named in the *Eighteenth Brumaire* as the moment when the innovator is forced to call upon his past to provide him with slogans and costumes for his new historical act, *die neue Weltgeschichtsszene*. Although this may be done 'anxiously', from insecurity, the function of translating the revolution into reality is achieved when the old language can be totally discarded and the new made independent. Although Marx's use of the concept of language masks and assumed theatrical roles is largely metaphorical, he is talking also about the real use in 1789 of slogans and titles from the Roman Republic to describe the aims of the new revolution, as too, perhaps, about his own need to find a new terminology. Thus the solution to crisis, which is described at the conclusion to the above passage, mirrors that apparently discovered in *The German Ideology* of 1846 of seeing imitation (in Marx's case parody) as a condition of crisis, and finding the solution to crisis in the abandonment of imitation.

The break with Young Hegelian methods of analysis was suggested in *The German Ideology* in passages such as 'not criticism but revolution is the driving force of history and also of religion, philosophy and all other types of history'. Language was to have a new performative function in revolution, and metaphor and symbol, common in parodistic language, were to be replaced by facts and figures. The use of parody, had also to be followed by social change to be attributed a performative function. By this *post hoc* method of judging the effect of parody suggested by Marx in 1852, the role of parody as a constituent of crisis in the chapters of *The German Ideology* written before the section on Feuerbach may also be said to have preceded change. There, ironically, a condition for parody to play a role in change was that it (parody) must cease for this change to be realised.

It cannot be claimed with any certainty that Marx was suggesting in the *Eighteenth Brumaire* that language and parodistic language could intervene in the development of material history. Marx speaks only of justifying the use of older slogans from a *post hoc* position: history will prove them to be either a prelude to revolution or farce. The success of the performative effect of intentional parody can also not be predicted. Although parody may be described as working in a dialectical manner in the supersession of an older text, by juxtaposing it with a 'contradictory' text and making a new text from the old, parody can only be attributed a role in freeing Marx from the terminology and methods of the Young Hegelians after the event and after he has exchanged parody for another, more direct style. In the *Eighteenth Brumaire* Marx designates social change[16] as determining the demarcation of breaks in ideology and the creation of new theories. Althusser, as Callinicos claims in *Althusser's Marxism*[17] also eventually (in *Lenin and Philosophy* and later works) 'abandons epistemology', in the sense of reducing it to a reflection of class struggle and the social conditions of history and the epistemological break to a symptom of social change. But we have also suggested that when Althusser moves Marx's break from Hegel from 1845 to 1870 there is little left of the mature Marxian problematic of which to search for symptoms in earlier works such as the *Eighteenth Brumaire*. The importance, even autonomy, of these individual works should not, moreover, be underrated. For it is their role in establishing Marx's mature works which (especially in the 'absence' of the latter!) must retain our interest.

Marx makes the nature of his break with Hegel quite clear in the
Eighteenth Brumaire. In quoting Hegel in the opening sentence as
having said that history repeats itself, Marx aligns him with an outdated theory, causing Hegel to sound like his enemies in the historical
school, for whom there was nothing new under the sun. Marx's
rhetorical skill in putting a thought into opposition to his own
argument by aligning it with a thought which has already fallen from
favour, is already in evidence in his alignment of Bauer with the
conservative Hegel in 1844. By this means Marx's own arguments are
made to appear more radically different from his target's. In claiming
that Hegel had forgotten to add that history repeats itself as farce,
Marx also introduces the idea of a 'break' into the concept of recurring
history. In the course of his argument in the *Eighteenth Brumaire* it
becomes clear that the break introduced after the farcical repetition of
history may be partial or total. Those imitations of older historical
periods which precede change or contribute to the crisis preceding it,
introduce a break which makes potential farce into a productive and
critical form of imitation. It is interesting to speculate on whether, or
to what extent, Marx was being ironic in criticising Hegel's philosophy
of history in 'making good' its omissions by juxtaposing Hegel's own
dialectical concept of supersession with the study of material history.
It could even be suggested, in other words, that Marx implies in the
Eighteenth Brumaire that Hegel had forgotten to add the dialectic
to the analysis of material history.

In 1852 Marx develops the concept of an 'historical break', or
revolution, in the forces of production, to 'supersede' Hegel's
dialectic, and to translate the idealist concept of supersession itself into
one applicable to the analysis of historical materialism. Yet, to some
extent, Marx also remains limited by his parodistic use of Hegel in the
Eighteenth Brumaire to an analysis of the forms and rhetoric of
Revolution, and to the metaphoric description of the nature of innovation: though the present is analysed in terms of class relations, its
past is not subjected to a rigorous materialist analysis. Thus the
Hegelian dialectic is placed in a new material context, and the past
made to serve the present without its own presuppositions being made
the subject of material analysis. As with the parodistic imitation of past
periods the service provided by the past to the present is only
temporary. In the Hegelian dialectic the 'negation of the negation' had
pointed away from one form of the idea to the next. When applied to
material history it might seem to bring with it this tendency and the
'false teleology' of Hegel's description on the *Philosophy of History*

of the realisation of the idea by itself. Yet when applied by Marx to material history and combined with the concept of a material break the dialectic becomes restricted to the description of material fact. It cannot impose categories but only describe them. Similarly, the revolutionary nature of some types of parody can only be known *post hoc*.

Marx's use of the metaphor of history as farce in the *Eighteenth Brumaire* serves a positive function in bringing the analysis of material history as a process of change together with the analysis of 'dialectical' parody. But it is also symptomatic of a negative tendency in that work to conceal the exact role of the Hegelian dialectic in the analysis of material history. Parody itself might be said to have played a role in the transformation of the Hegelian philosophy of history in the *Eighteenth Brumaire* but it cannot be used to complete the transformation or to prove it right. We have argued that Marx's own change from the methods of the Young Hegelians to the new theory of historical materialism was seen itself born in a situation of crisis similar to that described in the *Eighteenth Brumaire*, of having to find a new 'terminology', sometimes through parody, for its break with the past. But, as has been seen in that case, parody had to be dropped for change to lead to something new.

Parody plays an ambiguous role in the *Eighteenth Brumaire* in representing both a method for replacing Hegel's philosophy of history and a metaphor for the negative imitation of 1789 in 1848 and for Louis Napoleon's repetition of Napoleon's conversion of the Republic to an Empire. The *Eighteenth Brumaire* concludes by comparing Friedrich Wilhelm IV's support for the instigation of the cult of the Holy Cloak in Trier in 1844 (despite scientific evidence that the relic was false) to Louis Napoleon's revival of the cult of Napoleon I with his assumption of the imperial cloak. The farcical nature of Louis Napoleon's repetition of history is emphasised by the addition of the image of the statue of Napoleon falling in horror from its pedestal at the investiture of his imitation. In Marx's new view neither parody nor imitation can flatter: this ironic postscript to the description of the retrograde revival of the past puts the question of authority raised by Marx's earliest works into yet another light: not only is the imitation of older traditions and their use as authorities condemned as potentially farcical and reactionary, but the concept of progress in material history makes the imitation of history by definition a limitation on its process and the source of contradictions from which new crises and breaks may result. In the works following 1846 in which parody is seen as accompanying discontinuity in history, it is itself made secondary to other methods of criticism and to the analysis of the material forces of production in history.

For Marx the Hegelian dialectic was a mystified dialectic. Particular elements of this 'mystified' dialectic, such as the negation of the negation and the universal nature of the goal, were, as Hegel himself realised, also characteristic of irony. Marx's rejection of Hegel's mystified dialectic in the *Eighteenth Brumaire* is also, it has been noted, accompanied by a rejection of the ironic but non-dialectical reflective parody of his earlier works, the object of which had not been any other material subject but himself, his ideas or his models. Hegel's own concept of irony is not discussed in the early works of Marx which we have looked at; but when Marx uses Romantic irony (that is, reflective, self-perpetuating irony) in the works of 1837, he holds, as has been seen, a dislike for Hegel's system and a preference for the philosophies of Kant and Fichte. Fichte's *Wissenschaftslehre* had been praised by Friedrich Schlegel (with Goethe's *Wilhelm Meister* and the French Revolution) as one of the greatest events of present times. Schlegel's concept of cosmic irony, as a means to freedom for the particular self in heightened self-consciousness in the 'universalisation' of itself, has been put by some critics into the context of Fichte's description of the raising to self-consciousness of the self in the universal self. Irony, like the dialectic involved in Fichte's system, was seen by Schlegel as working by means of a conflict of identities having the appearance of opposites, as of the self and the non-self.[18]

Schlegel's work on irony was developed by K.W.F. Solger and by Hegel,[19] who criticised, however, the limited nature of the Fichtean dialectic and the theories of irony related to it. Solger's irony, on the other hand, Hegel calls 'dialectical'. Solger saw irony as a way of viewing both tragedy and comedy as the conflict between ideals and reality in society. Hegel made Solger's concept of irony the basis for a description of irony as parallel to the negation of the negation in his dialectic. In this way the ironist's use of a method of rejecting a false argument by means of contradiction in order to come to the opposite point of view to the opponent's argument (in the older sense of Socratic irony) was likened to that moment in history when progress was preceded by the negation of the negation. Though Marx like Heine had also used parody dialectically in this way, Marx's application of the dialectic to history in 1852 was accompanied as we have seen by his rejection of parody for more scientific methods. In 1852 Marx uses parody metaphorically to condemn repetition in history, rather than as an image of progress. Hence both Hegel's idealist dialectic and the concept of dialectical irony are critically re-worked in that text. Friedrich Schlegel had once defined irony as a form of 'genial self-parody', and Marx also shifts the emphasis in 1852 from the reflective nature of irony and parody in history, to the critical control of other events by the observer, and from the idea in history to the development of the means of production by man. The imitation of the Roman Republic in 1789 is attributed not a reflective but a tactical role: conscious and successful parody is not a means to the preservation of a former type of consciousness on a higher level of self-knowledge (as irony had been for the Romantics) but a means to the transcendence of the past in its eventual rejection. Similarly, those events termed parodies (in a pejorative sense) because of the unproductive nature of their imitation of the past, do not designate history transcending itself in progressing through supersession of the thesis, or the negation of the negation, but the necessary poverty of these reflective processes in material history.

In rejecting the Young Hegelian use of parody as a method of criticism, and in rejecting the 'idealist' Hegelian dialectic, Marx also implies a rejection of the Fichtean dialectic and of Romantic irony, and of Kant's belief in the use of other such forms of poetic *ingenium* as a way to knowledge, though, as we have seen, he retains belief in Kant's praise of knowledge which breaks its own limits.

Marx's analysis of art in the unpublished Introduction to the *Grundrisse*, of 1857, translates Schiller's essay on the naive and sentimental into terms of material production. There Marx explains the continued charm of Greek art (the naive) in the sentimental, modern age as resting in the knowledge of historical change which modern man gains through his recognition of the fact that Greek art represents an earlier, now lost stage in the development of material history. In these terms Greek art does not only represent the 'childhood of man' in terms of the history of art, but also in terms of material production. But here Marx must leap from Greek art to society, and to do this he reverts to Schiller's and Hegel's assumption that there was an unusual, now lost 'naive' harmony between art and society as well as a naive relationship of man to production in the Greek world. For Marx distinguished Greek society, the childhood of modern man, from the present age by describing its modes of production and consumption as being based on the principle of use value: modern society, on the other hand, has developed a more sophisticated, and 'alienating' system of exchange value.

It must be emphasised that Marx rejected this 1857 Introduction in 1859 as too abstract, and left it unpublished because of this. As an aesthetic Marx's explanation of the continuing charm of Greek art is not sufficient, and involves, as argued above, assumptions still based in Schiller's idealist aesthetic, as well as the unfounded, or, at least, unexplained, jump from aesthetic to social questions, from the work of art to the mode of production of utility or exchangeable goods. Marx's explanation of how Greek art can still be understood in such changed historical circumstances as exists in the modern industrial world is tendentiously directed towards arguing for the necessity of comprehending historical change in the material world, but the relationship of art to that world is never clearly defined.

Postscript

In the wake of the recent rejection of the concept of art as *Widerspiegelung* (reflection), as supposing a static rather than a dialectical or dynamic relationship between society and art, parody — as a way of distorting the image of reality perceived by readers and other writers and of breaking from the past — has drawn attention to itself yet again as a weapon in political writing. Very little discussion of the limitations of parody in this role, which Marx and Engels encountered in the 1840s, has, however, accompanied this revival. For the modernists wanting to destroy the restriction of art to the process of imitation, parody (as a meta-fiction) appears to prove this possible, while also showing the centrality of the artist's perception of reality to his message. Parody, in this way, is taken to be a means of talking about a relationship of art to reality which has been freed from the limits of mimesis. As David Roberts writes in his study of Heinrich Mann,[20] 'Parody is an integral part of any history of *mimesis* in European literature. Parody, the imitation of art, is the critique of the presentation or imitation of reality in art.'

Heinz Brüggeman, in his study of Brecht's theory of literature,[21] rejects the concept of art as *Widerspiegelung*, as reflecting the conservative mind of the closed society, and contrasts it with the idea of parody as the negation, in literature, of existing reality. Parody in Brüggeman's sense is less the polyphonic, ambiguous restructuring of past works which we find, for example, in models such as *Don Quixote*, than the satiric confrontation of the reader and the book, and of literature with reality. And yet Brecht's parody, like Heine's, does have the character of irony as well as of satire — renewing the past in the act of destroying it, as in the *Aufhebung* of the negation of the negation in the Hegelian dialectic which Hegel himself had once compared to irony. Though such parody creates for itself the problem of remaining attached to that which it wishes to eliminate, it also establishes change within continuity in the literary tradition and a multiplicity of images within a single text characteristic of great art. Such parody also breaks from the formulation of disputes as argument and counter-argument, which is, as David Roberts has suggested elsewhere,[22] characteristic of the 'closed society'. Thus it also avoids the dialogue between reality and counter-reality found in simple forms of satire. Whether this 'counter-reality' takes the form of an ideal (as in Schiller's definition of satire), or of any other form of corrective, such dialogues are of a 'static' rather than a dialectical character.

Marx's imitation of the Young Hegelian use of parody as a counter-argument in the early 1840s restricted his criticism, as we have seen, to communication within the closed group which he was attacking. Only when the conditions making that closed discussion necessary — such as censorship, an antiquated terminology, and an unchanging political and social structure — had themselves been transformed, could the new and dialectical method of argument be put into practice. Marx too had argued in 1852 that only a revolution in social conditions could create ground for a new literature in Europe. But he was not necessarily convinced of the supremacy of non-mimetic art over mimetic art, or of its power to change society, for not only did he use the term parody deprecatingly, to describe the farcical imitation of a past historical period, but he also left it and irony for more direct and scientific language, only to return to it occasionally, as in the case of the diatribe against Herr Vogt in 1860.

For Brüggeman, however, some political parody can have the function of changing reality. This type of parody he calls (after Korsch's concept of *geistige Aktion*) *verändernde Praxis*, Praxis which transforms or changes its object. Brüggeman considers this form of performative argument as going hand in hand with the rejection of art as mimesis. For Brecht, Brüggeman argues, this implies a relationship of *Wechselwirkung* between literature and life. Yet it is also clear, that to be more than counter-argument, the parody must not only be used to criticise reality — and change it — but must also reflect the parodist in the process of writing, making his assumptions about his activity known. Parody must be ironic and self-reflective as well as satiric in order to create more than an argument opposed to a counter-argument and to serve a dialectical and innovative function, as well as a performative, 'practical' role. This, however, is the problem: purely

satiric parody, which has a much better chance of being understood
by a general public and of having some impact on their lives, is
generally of the static argument versus counter-argument type, while
ironic parody, which may be used to reflect the parodist's views on the
relationship of literature to reality, as to other literary works, is, as
Marx knew, a much more complex and indirect form of communication
and an indirect or subtle means of changing a particular view of
reality. Though Brüggeman would see Brecht as a true follower of
Marx in his aesthetic, the concerns of the writer – like the character
of his audience – were very different from those of the Marx the social
philosopher. Thus, while Brecht continued to use parody in his epic
theatre, Marx and Engels argued out their debate on the effectiveness
of parody as *verändernde Praxis* early in their work, in the 1840s,
before leaving it for other issues and more direct methods of criticism.

Notes

1.   As mentioned earlier, Goethe's *Zahme Xenien* against Pustkuchen are
also quoted in *Die grossen Männer*, but not with the explicit intention (as in
1837) of defending Goethe, but of attacking Kinkel: Dietze Ausgabe, vol. 8,
p. 243. 'Hat doch der Walfisch sein Laus/Kann ich auch mein haben'.

2.   Ibid., p. 249.

3.   Dietz Ausgabe, vol. 8, p. 276.

4.   MEGA I/1 (2), pp. 85-6.

5.   Karl Marx and Fr. Engels, *Werke*, Dietz Verlag, vol. 8, p. 115.

6.   MEGA I/5, p. 29.

7.   It is this negative form taken by parody that critical dialectical parody
serves to supersede in initiating change.

8.   Chr. D. Grabbe, *Scherz, Satire, Ironie und tiefere Bedeutung*, Reclam,
Stuttgart, 1970, p. 31.

9.   *The Correspondence of Alexander Pope*, George Sherburn (ed.), Oxford,
1956, p. 71. Quoted by Ian Donaldson, *The World Upside Down*, Oxford, 1970,
p. 158.

10.   MEGA I/2, p. 62.

11.   Hook, p. 135.

12.   MEGA I/2, p. 65.

13.   M. Rose, *Die Parodie: Eine Funktion der biblischen Sprache in Heines
Lyrik*, p. 83 ff.

14.   Marx uses the term parody in this sense in the *Eighteenth Brumaire*
and Heine in *Deutschland. Ein Wintermärchen*: Caput XVII, '. . . Schliesse die
Schauspielhäuser,/Wo man die Vorzeit parodiert –/Komme du bald, O Kaiser –'.

15.   *Basic Writings on Politics and Philosophy*, Lewis S. Feuer (ed.), New
York, 1959, p. 320. And Dietz Verlag, *Werke*, vol. 8, p. 115.

16.   Specifically, the class struggles in France. The *Eighteenth Brumaire*
has been called the continuation of the 'Klassenkämpfe in Frankreich. 1848-
1850'. See *Werke*, Dietz Verlag, vol. 8, Preface, XI.

17.   Alex Callinicos, *Althusser's Marxism*, London, 1976, p. 88.

18.   See I. Strohschneider-Kohrs, *Die Romantische Ironie in Theorie und Gestaltung*, Tübingen, 1960; D. Muecke, *The Compass of Irony*, London, 1969; Wayne C. Booth, *The Rhetoric of Irony*, Chicago, 1974.

19.   See S. Kierkegaard, *The Concept of Irony*, 1841.

20.   David Roberts, *Artistic Consciousness and Political Conscience, The Novels of Heinrich Mann, 1900-1938*, Bern, 1971.

21.   Heinz Brüggemann, *Literarische Technik und soziale Revolution*, Hamburg, 1973.

22.   In the Symposium on Parody, Humanities Research Centre, Australian National University, Canberra, July 1976.

6.1 CONCLUSION

Functions of Parody in the Works of Marx and Engels from 1837 to 1852

In the fragments of the unfinished novel of 1837 *Scorpion und Felix*, Marx had described both history and his novel as victims of the law of progression from the sublime to the ridiculous. Not only had Marx's novel been an epigonal attempt to revive the Romantic comic novel, but Marx's description of history as the alternation of the sublime with the ridiculous had also been culled from works of contemporary writers such as Heine. Both the idea and the practice of the novel, joined with the concept of history as time running down, led to the use of parody as a mirror to the absurdity of the ridiculous in history. Similarly, the satires on Hegel had used parody as a form of counter-argument to Hegel's arguments against Kant and Fichte: it had led to no new arguments, but back to a defence of the object of its target's criticism.

In *The Holy Family* of 1844-5 Bruno Bauer's use of parody as a tool to attack the critics of Young Hegelian philosophy and to present new arguments in a covert, indirect manner (which Engels had also used in his satirical defence of Bauer in 1842) is used to attack Bauer himself. Here parody is made a tool of satire. Yet although parody in *The Holy Family* is not merely used as counter-argument but as part of a satirical and critical attack on the Young Hegelians from a new Feuerbachian position, parody is still used *ad hominem* against Bauer, as a reflection on his own use of parody. A contradiction begins to emerge in *The Holy Family* in Marx's and Engels' simultaneous rejection of Bauer's philosophy and imitation of Bauer's methods in the continued use of his parodistic method. The crisis born of this dilemma becomes evident in *The German Ideology* of 1845-6, in the change from the use of parody in the early chapters on the Young Hegelians to the more direct style of the chapter on Feuerbach. Parody is now used not only to attack Bauer and other Young Hegelians but also to escape from their methods.

In 1852, in the *Eighteenth Brumaire*, revolutionary history is described as dialectical, but static repetitious history as farce: similarly parody which precedes change is dialectical. Marx also introduces the essay with verbal parody when he refunctions Hegel's philosophy of history to argue that repetitions in history are to be understood as farce, but the metaphorical use of the word parody to describe this farce expresses scepticism too about the over-use of it as a *method of criticism*. Significantly, Marx now no longer uses parody to the degree he had in 1844-5. The use of parody, after contributing to the crisis preceding the break from the Young Hegelians, can never again be the end in itself it had been in *The Holy Family*. Bauer's parodistic method had been confronted with itself, and the dilemma of serving the new theory of historical materialism, and been rejected.

Literary parody, as it was, for example, understood by the readers of Cervantes, had had the function of mocking accepted authorities and superseding older traditions through making them part of the text of the literary parody by means of quotation or imitation. Yet for Marx in his juvenilia of 1837 parody had been the last recourse open to the epigone. It had not, in its imitative, second-hand form, led the young author to a path out of this impasse and Marx had, by his admission, given up the writing of verse and other forms of imaginative literature towards the end of 1837. As for Engels a few years later, imaginative writing now gave way to philosophy. Marx's juvenilia had remained entrenched in a static and partly repressed conflict of the young author with both figures of authority within his immediate environment and with the use of literary models as authorities to be imitated rather than changed. Typical of these young works is Marx's use of parody in satire to defend authorities – as in the defence of Kant against Hegel in the epigrams on Hegel. The role of censorship in reinforcing authority is also important in maintaining the use of parody in the work of the Young Hegelians, as a way of 'smuggling' ideas past the censor but also in creating a closed circle of initiates to counteract the voice of authority in the closed society.

Marx's break with the Young Hegelian mentor Bauer in 1844, and with his methods in 1846, was one of the first explicit breaks with a past authority in their joint work. It was all the more significant for being accompanied by the development of the new theory of historical materialism. Parody had not only served to silence the direct discussion of material problems in *The Holy Family* and *The German Ideology* by expanding those works to the 21 *Bogen* necessary to escape the statutory pre-censorship, but the writing of the philosophical books had delayed the discussion of economic problems for which Marx had signed a contract with Leske in 1845. After that contract was cancelled in 1846 it was then more than ten years before the *Grundrisse* were written. This is but one example of the indirect silencing effect of actual censorship on Marx's writing overlooked by Althusser and other critics when discussing the silences in Marx's texts. Further problems with publishing following Louis Napoleon's *coup* of 1851 and Marx's move to London also of course contributed to the delay of the mature works on economic questions of material history.

In practice, parody is used in the *Eighteenth Brumaire* as a tool of satire as well as a method of productively recombining and refunctioning philosophical concepts and suggesting material changes. After 1852 Marx continued to be accused of a sin of his youth, of misquoting and distorting texts. While the opening sentence of the *Eighteenth Brumaire* had used parody deliberately to distort Hegel's philosophy of history, many of the later misquotations appear to have been made less with the intention of comic effect than with distinguishing Marx's position in the debate from that of his opponents. In the works of 1844 to 1846 Marx had often misquoted his opponents (as well as his allies) or − as in the biblical parody used to mock Bauer and Stirner − put their words into the context of well-known texts such as the Bible, to mock the 'mystifying' effect of their words and to make them even more ambiguous through their parodistic juxtaposition with the sacred text. Parody had also been used to reduce the opponents to words, to reify them in reducing them to a concrete version of their text. Yet this had also led Marx and Engels into becoming the victims of their own over-use of parody. Only when parody was able to be used to liberate Marx and Engels from what had almost become a fetish of Bauer's method was it able to be used to free them from their former models and own earlier works. Dialectical parody, parody producing change, also effected a change in the parodist and his audience, an element not yet discussed in detail in this study. The changing historical context of the writings of Marx and Engels made it not illogical for them to condemn others (as in *Die großen Männer des Exils* of 1852) for reading and believing writings they themselves had once read and praised. Finally, the double censorship of the early works of Marx and Engels, in their own time and in ours, makes a connection between their contemporary readership and ourselves, between their methods of reading texts and ours important. The aim of the following brief note on the relationship of the reader to the book is thus not only to summarise the general functions of Marx's parody in his own time,[1] or to comment on its reception and interpretation by his contemporaries, but to refer back to the problems facing us today in reading Marx and Engels.

Note

1.   I have kept a detailed explanation of the functions of parody, and of the history of its usage in world literature, for a separate study, *Parody//Meta-Fiction*, which is to be published by Croom Helm early in 1979.

6.2 THE READER AND THE BOOK

One of the central functions of the use of parody in Marx's works has been seen to be the liberation of the author from his authorities and their terminology. Though Kant had seen this as a liberation from preconceptions of thought and Hegel from historical periods, Marx had to see this as liberation from both his liberal mentors and their enemy the censor. The role of parody in contributing to the crisis preceding actual change (by, for example, being both the method of revision and a hindrance to radical change) has already been discussed, but the specific ways in which parody may, theoretically, effect a change to *parole* language, have still to be outlined. As a general semantic rule it may be maintained that the transference of a lexeme from one context to another will affect its meaning in some manner. Through displacing a text from its original context, through juxtaposing it with another text or by changing its context through omission, addition, or other similar methods which result in distortion or incongruity, parody may obtain this result of changing the meaning of a text as well as its form. Often parody may use a technique of lexical transference similar to metaphor, which is one of the most creative elements in language, as linguists such as the Prague linguist Jan Mukarovsky, have indicated. But parody may also provide a new perspective on a work by foregrounding (in the sense used by Mukarovsky, but also in the sense of revealing what is concealed in fiction) both the role of the parodist as a decoder (or reader) of the text being parodied and the role of the reader outside the text as the decoder of the parody as a whole as well as of the text being parodied within it. Thus the parody not only puts the reader in the position of having to make a critical choice between the texts offered him, but also of having to contrast or match the presuppositions of the texts with his own world. In this way parody may indirectly function as performative speech in effecting a change in the world of the reader.

In changing either the meaning of the text being parodied and its structure, or the assumptions of the reader about the texts offered to him to decode, the successful parodist may 'free' himself from the terminology and presuppositions of the author of the parodied text and his audience. The imitation of form is then a means to the end of initiating change in a text. Initially the parodist may quote from the

151

text to be imitated (as Marx quotes Hegel at the beginning of the *Eighteenth Brumaire*: 'Hegel says somewhere . . .'), to elicit expectations in his audience for that text, as well as to establish a contrast between the text and the distortion which will follow. But dialectical parody will not return to the quotation of the parodied text in its conclusion: *Don Quixote* begins, for example, as the parody of the romance and ends, as history as shown, as a preview of the modern novel. This pattern might also be applied to *The German Ideology*, but what is also common to both works is the discontinuity accompanying change, as well as a defence of discontinuity against the continuity of imitation, which follows in defence of their practice. Perhaps a greater significance might be given the numerous quotations from, allusions to, and satirical refunctioning of Cervantes' *Don Quixote* to be found in *The German Ideology* in view of the functional similarity of parody in the two works. But the analysis of the functions of parody in Marx's work must not obscure the importance of material factors; for the experience of France in 1843 as well as social events in Germany in the *Vormärz* had, together with the problem of liberating their style from the Young Hegelians, preceded the change in Marx's and Engels' work in 1846. Both the subject and the method of Marx's philosophy changed in the period of which the chapter on Feuerbach in *The German Ideology* is a new symptom. With this change parody also became freed from the reflective function it had had from the juvenilia up to the satiric attacks on the Young Hegelians, so that it could be used for a wider audience than that initiated into the philosophy of the Young Hegelians. In the later works, when it does appear, parody is used to contrast fiction with reality (as when Hegel's idealist philosophy is ironically contrasted with material reality in 1852), and the book with the reader (as Cervantes' parody had in *Don Quixote*), to re-establish a contrast and dialectic between the reader and the book which could lend a performative function to the parody.

Marx's early juvenilia suffered both from the lack of critical editing and a critical readership. The parody used in them is typically ironic and self-reflective as well as imitative of the Romantics. It is the works of the early 1840s in which the dilemma accompanying the use of parody for a small and restricted audience begins to develop into crisis. The widening of Marx's and Engels' readership occurs both under the threat of censorship and together with their limiting attacks on Bauer's over-use of literary allusion and parody. Perhaps one of the most central issues accompanying the development of a concept of dialectical parody in the work of Marx and Engels is that of the relationship of both authors to the use of literary authorities and to the figures of both benign and malign authority around them.

Here Parody has been described as a symptom of this battle against authority and of an epistemological crisis in Marx and Engels' *oeuvre*. But, looking back over Marx's works, it can also be seen on the level of biography as a symptom of the liberation of the present from the past, and, in the *Eighteenth Brumaire*, as a means of transferring the language of the past into the present. Together with the censorship which it served to evade, it restricted Marx's work to an initiated audience. And an understanding of the material conditions in which parody had to be used in the 1840s, together with a critical reading of the 'silenced' reactions to those conditions concealed in the juvenilia, are important for a proper understanding of the place of Marx's poetic works in both his biography and in the history of his period. But such esoteric subjects also require readers (initiated and un-initiated in the reading of esoteric texts) patient enough to follow the young Marx across the borders dividing literature, philosophy, and the social sciences.

BIBLIOGRAPHY

Editions: Marx and Engels. Works

Marx, Karl und Engels, Friedrich, *Gesamtausgabe* (MEGA), ed. Marx-Engels-Institute, Moscow, Frankfurt-am-Main, 1927 ff

Marx, Karl und Engels, Friedrich, *Gesamtausgabe* (New MEGA), ed. Institut fur Marxismus-Leninismus, Berlin, 1975 ff

Marx, Karl und Engels, Friedrich, *Werke*, Dietz Verlag, Berlin, 1960

Marx, Karl and Engels, Friedrich, *Collected Works*, Lawrence and Wishart, London, 1975 ff

Marx and Engels, *Basic Writings on Politics and Philosophy*, ed. Lewis S. Feuer, New York, 1959

Writings of the Young Marx on Philosophy and Society, ed. Lloyd D. Easton and Kurt H. Guddat, New York, 1967

Marx. Early Writings, ed. Lucio Colletti (transl. R. Livingstone and G. Benton), Middlesex, 1975

Engels: Ludwig Feuerbach and the End of Classical German Philosophy, ed. C.P. Dutt, New York, 1967

Other Primary Texts

Aeschylus, *Complete Works*, ed. G. Murray, London, 1952

Aristophanes, *Complete Works* (transl. P. Dickinson), London, 1970

Aristotle, *Rhetorics*, ed. Keith Erikson, New Jersey, 1974

Arnim, Achim von und Brentano, Clemens, *Des Knaben Wunderhorn*, München, 1966

Bauer, Bruno, *Allgemeine Literaturzeitung*, 1843-4, 2nd edn., Charlottenberg, 1847

Börne, Ludwig, *Sämtliche Schriften*, 5 vols, Düsseldorf, 1964

Chamisso, Adalbert von, *Werke*, ed. Tardel, Leipzig, 1907

Die Bibel, nach der Übersetzung Dr Martin Luthers, Halle, 1811

Eichendorff, Jos. von, *Sämtliche Werke*, Regensburg, 1962

Feuerbach, Ludwig, *Sämtliche Werke*, Stuttgart, 1903 f

Freiligrath, Ferdinand, *Gesammelte Dichtungen*, 6 vols, Stuttgart, 1871

Goethe, Joh. W., *Werke*, 14 vols., Hamburg, 1964

Grabbe, Christian D., *Werke*, 6 vols., Darmstadt, 1960

Gutzkow, Karl, *Werke*, Leipzig, 1912

Hegel, G.W.Fr., *Sämtliche Werke*, 20 vols., Stuttgart, 1958

_____ *Die Hegelsche Linke*, ed., K. Löwith, Stuttgart, 1962

Heine, Heinrich, *Sämtliche Werke*, ed. E. Elster, 7 vols., Leipzig, 1893 f

_____ *Historisch-kritische Ausgabe der Werke*, ed. M. Windfuhr, Düsseldorf, 1974 ff

Herder, Joh. G., *Sämtliche Werke*, 33 vols., Berlin, 1913

Hermand, Jost Ed., *Das junge Deutschland*, Stuttgart, 1967

_____ *Der deutsche Vormärz*, Stuttgart, 1969

Herwegh, Georg, *Werke*, Berlin, 1909

Humboldt, Wilhelm von, *The Limits of State Action*, ed. J.W. Burrow, Cambridge, 1969

Immermann, Karl, *Werke*, 5 vols., Leipzig, 1906

Kant, Immanuel, *Anthropologie*, Leipzig, 1799

_____ *Werke*, ed. Reimer, Berlin 1910 ff

_____ *Political Writings*, ed. Reiss, Cambridge, 1970

Klopstock, F.G., *Ausgewählte Werke*, Stuttgart, 1869

Lessing, G.E., *Gesammelte Werke*, 10 vols., Berlin, 1956

Menzel, Wolfgang, *Das Literaturblatt*, 1834-6, Stuttgart

Novalis, *Schriften*, Stuttgart, 1960 ff

Obermann, Karl (ed.), *Flugblätter der Revolution. 1848/9*, Berlin, 1970

Ovid, *Tristia*, ed. Georg Luck, Heidelberg, 1967

Petrarch, *Sonnets and Songs*, New York, 1946

Schiller, Friedrich, *Werke*, Nationalausgabe, ed. Petersen und Fricke, Weimar, 1943 ff

Schlegel, August von, *Kritische Schriften*, Main, 1966

Schlegel, Friedrich, *Lucinde*, Stuttgart, 1964

Shakespeare, William, *Complete Works*, The Arden Shakespeare, London, 1964 ff

Strauss, D.F., *Das Leben Jesu*, 2 vols., Darmstadt, 1969

Sue, Eugene, *Les mystères de Paris*, Paris, 1843

Weerth, Georg, *Sämtliche Werke*, Berlin, 1957

Weitling, Wilhelm, *Das Evangelium des armen Sünders*, ed. Wolf Schäfer, Hamburg, 1971

Wienbarg, Ludolf, *Ästhetische Feldzüge*, Berlin, 1964

Secondary Literature

Abrams, M.H., *The Mirror and the Lamp*, New York, 1953

Adams, Henry P., *Karl Marx in his Earlier Writings*, London, 1940

Althusser, Louis, *For Marx* (transl. Brewster), Middlesex, 1969

_____ *Reading Capital* (transl. Brewster), London, 1970

_____ *Lenin and Philosophy* (transl. Brewster), London, 1971

_____ *Essays in Self-Criticism* (transl. G. Lock), London, 1976

Andreas, Bert und Mönke, Wolfgang, 'Neue Daten zur "Deutschen Ideologie" ', in *Archiv für Sozialgeschichte*, vol. 8, Part 1, 1968, pp. 5-152

Avineri, Shlomo, *The Social and Political Thought of Karl Marx*, Cambridge, 1968

―――― *Hegel's Theory of the Modern State*, Cambridge, 1972

Berlin, Isaiah, *Karl Marx*, London, 1972

Blumenberg, Werner, *Karl Marx*, London, 1972

Bodi, Leslie, *Tauwetter in Wien*, Frankfurt-am-Main, 1977

Böhme, S., *Grundlage und Methodik der Literaturbetrachtung bei Marx und Engels* (Diss.), Berlin, 1954

Brewster, Ben, 'Althusser and Bachelard', in *Theoretical Practice*, 1971 (3), p. 25 ff

Brüggemann, Heinz, *Literarische Technik und soziale Revolution*, Hamburg, 1973

Brunschwig, Henri, *Enlightenment and Romanticism in Eighteenth Century Prussia* (1947) (transl. Frank Jellinek), Chicago, 1974

Buchbinder, Reinhard, *Bibelzitate, Bibelanspielungen, Bibelparodien, theologische Vergleiche und Analogien bei Marx und Engels*, Berlin, 1976

Callinicos, Alex, *Althusser's Marxism*, London, 1976

Cornforth, Maurice, *Materialism and the Dialectic Method*, 4th edn., New York, 1975

Cornu, Auguste, *Karl Marx et Friedrich Engels. Leur vie et leur oeuvre*, vol. 1, Paris, 1955

Dahnke, Hans Dietrich, *Karl Marx und die politische Lyrik des Vormärz*, Berlin, 1953

Demetz, Peter, *Marx, Engels und die Dichter*, Frankfurt-am-Main, 1969

Donaldson, Ian, *The World Upside Down. Comedy from Jonson to Fielding*, Oxford, 1970

Eagleton, Terry, *Marxism and Literary Criticism*, London, 1976

―――― *Criticism and Ideology*, London, 1976

Erckenbrecht, Ulrich, *Marxs materialistische Speachtheorie* (transl. Kronburg), 1973

Fehervary, H., 'Marx und Hölderlin in der DDR', in B. Grimm and J. Hermand (eds.), *Basis*, vol. 5 (1975), pp. 55-64

Floren, Angel, *Literature and Marxism. A Controversy by Marxist Critics*, New York, 1938

Grandjonc, Jacques, *Marx et les communistes allemands 1844*, Paris, 1974

Gurvitch, Georges, 'Saint-Simon et Karl Marx', in *Revue Internationale de Philosophie*, vol. 14 (1960), pp. 399-416

Hermand, Jost, *Von Mainz nach Weimar, 1793-1919*, Stuttgart, 1969

_____ *Streitobjekt Heine. Ein Forschungsbericht, 1945-1975*, Frankfurt-am-Main, 1975

Hillmann, Günther, *Marx und Hegel*, Frankfurt-am-Main, 1966

Hodges, D., 'The Young Marx: A Reappraisal', in *Philosophical and Phenomenological Research*, December, 1966

Hook, Sidney, *From Hegel to Marx*, Michigan, 1962

Hömberg, Walter, *Zeitgeist und Ideenschmuggel*, Stuttgart, 1975

Houben, H.H., *Verbotene Literatur*, Hildersheim, 1965

Jaeggi, Urs., *Theoretische Praxis*, Frankfurt-am-Main, 1976

Jameson, Fredric, *Marxism and Form*, Princeton, 1971

Johnston, William M., 'Karl Marx's verse of 1836-1837 as a foreshadowing of his early philosophy', in *Journal of the History of Ideas*, April 1967, pp. 259 ff

Kamenka, Eugene, *The Philosophy of Ludwig Feuerbach*, London, 1970

_____ *The Ethical Foundations of Marxism*, 2nd edn., London, 1972

_____ 'Marxism and Ethics. A Reconsideration', in Shlomo Avineri (ed.), *Varieties of Marxism*, Jerusalem, 1975

Köster, Udo, *Literarischer Radikalismus*, Frankfurt-am-Main, 1972

Kreutzer, Leo, *Heine und der Kömmunismus*, Göttingen, 1970

Krieger, Leonard, *The German Idea of Freedom*, Chicago, 1972

_____ *Essays on the Theory of Enlightened Despotism*, Chicago, 1975

Kuhn, T.S., *The Structure of Scientific Revolutions*, Chicago, 1969

Künzli, Arnold, *Karl Marx. Eine Psychographie*, Zürich, 1966

Lacan, Jacques, *The Language of the Self* (transl. Anthony Wilden), New York, 1975

Lazarowicz, Klaus, *Verkehrte Welt*, Tübingen, 1963

Lecourt, Dominique, *Marxism and Epistemology* (transl. Ben Brewster), 1975

Lefebvre, Jean Pierre, 'Marx und Heine', in *Heinrich Heine. Streitbarer Humanist und volksverbundener Dichter*, Weimar Konferenz, Weimar, 1974

Levin, Michael, 'Marxism and Romanticism. Marx's debt to German Conservatism', in *Political Studies*, no. 22 (1974), pp. 400-13

Lifshitz, M., *The Philosophy of Art of Karl Marx* (1933) (transl. Ralph B. Winn), London, 1973

_____ *Karl Marx und die Ästhetik*, Dresden, 1960

Lukács, Georg, *Werke*, Neuwied, 1969

McLellan, David, *The Young Hegelians and Karl Marx*, London, 1969

_____ *Marx before Marxism*, Middlesex, 1972

Machackova, Vera, *Der junge Engels und die Literatur. 1838-1844*, Berlin, 1961

Macherey, Pierre, *Pour une Théorie de la production littéraire*, Paris, 1970

Marcus, S., *Engels, Manchester and the Working Class*, London, 1974

Marcuse, Herbert, *Eros and Civilization*, London, 1956

Mayer, Gustav, 'Marx und der zweite Teil der Posaune', 1916

Mehring, Franz, *Aus dem literarischen Nachlass von Karl Marx und Friedrich Engels*, 3 vols., Stuttgart, 1920

_____ *Aufsätze zur deutschen Literaturgeschichte*, Leipzig, 1960

_____ *Karl Marx. The Story of His Life* (1918), London, 1966

Meszaros, Istvan, *Marx's Theory of Alienation*, London, 1970

Moering, Michael, *Witz und Ironie in der Prosa Heinrich von Kleists*, München, 1972

Mommsen, Katharina, 'Heines lyrische Anfänge in Schatten der Karlsbader Beschlüsse', in Alexander von Bormann (ed.), *Wissen aus Erfahrungen*, Tübingen, 1976

Monas, Sidney, *The Third Section. Police and Society in Russia under Nicholas I*, Harvard, 1961

Mönke, Wolfgang, *Die heilige Familie. Zur ersten Gemeinschaftsarbeit von Karl Marx und Friedrich Engels*, Glashütten im Taunus, 1972

Monz, Heinz, *Karl Marx und Trier*, Trier, 1964

_____ *Karl Marx. Grundlagen der Entwicklung zu Leben und Werk*, Trier, 1973

Morawski, Stefan, 'The Aesthetic Views of Marx and Engels', in *Journal of Aesthetics and Art Criticism*, no. 28 (1969), p. 301 ff

Müllenbach, Herbert, *Die Entwicklung der Pressfreiheit in Preussen* (Diss.), Freiburg, 1935

Nicolaevsky, Boris and Maenchen-Helfen, Otto, *Karl Marx: Man and Fighter* (1935), Middlesex, 1976

Ollivier, Marcel, *Marx et Engels poètes*, Paris, 1935

Ollmann, Bertell, *Alienation*, Cambridge, 1971

Otto, Ulla, *Die literarische Zensur als Problem der Soziologie der Politik*, Stuttgart, 1968

Payne, Robert, *Marx*, New York, 1968

Plekhanov, G., *Art and Society*, London, 1953

Popper, Karl, *The Open Society and Its Enemies*, London, 1966

Prawer, S.S., 'What did Karl Marx think of Schiller?', in *German Life and Letters*, October 1975, pp. 122-37

_____ 'Mephisto and Old Nick', in Proceedings of the *English Goethe Society*, 1975

_____ *Marx and World Literature*, Oxford, 1976

Prevost, Claude, *Littérature, Politique, Idéologie*, Paris, 1973

Raddatz, Fritz J., *Marxismus und Literatur*, 3 vols., Beinbek, 1969

Radlik, Ute, 'Heine in der Zensur der Restaurationsepoche', in Jost Hermand and M. Windfuhr (eds.), *Literatur der Restaurationsepoche*, Stuttgart, 1970

Reeves, Nigel, 'Heine and the Young Marx', in *Oxford German Studies*, no. 7 (1973), p. 44 ff

Reisner, Hanns-Peter, *Literatur unter der Zensur. Die politische Lyrik des Vormärz*, Stuttgart, 1975

Roberts, David, *Artistic Consciousness and Political Conscience: The Novels of Heinrich Mann. 1900-1938*, Bern, 1971

Rose, Margaret, *Die Parodie. Eine Funktion der biblischen Sprache in Heines Lyrik*, Meisenheim, 1976

_____ ' "Adam der Erste" und das Verlagsverbot vom 8. Dezember 1841', in *Heine Jahrbuch*, 1975, pp. 70-6

_____ 'Althusser's symptomatic reading in the light of his "Essays in Self-Criticism" ' (unpublished)

Rosen, Zwi, *Bruno Bauer and Karl Marx*, The Hague, 1977

Schneider, Franz, *Pressefreiheit und politische Öffentlichkeit*, Neuwied, 1966

Solomon, Maynard (ed.), *Marxism and Art*, New York, 1973

Strauss, Leo, *Spinoza's Critique of Religion* (1930), New York, 1965

Swayze, Harold, *Political Control of Literature in the USSR. 1946-1959*, Cambridge (Mass.), 1962

Thomas, Rüdiger, 'Der unbekannte junge Marx', in *Der unbekannte junge Marx*, Mainz, 1973

Timpanaro, S., *The Freudian Slip. Psychoanalysis and Textual Criticism* (1974) (transl. Soper), London, 1976

Tucker, Robert, *Philosophy and Myth in Karl Marx* (2nd edn.), Cambridge, 1972

Victor, Walther, *Marx und Heine*, Berlin, 1952

Wilkie, Richard W., 'Karl Marx on Rhetoric', in *Philosophy and Rhetori Rhetoric*, no. 9/4 (Autumn 1976)

Wilpert, Gero. von, *Deutsches Dichterlexikon*, Stuttgart, 1963

Windfuhr, Manfred, 'Heine und Hegel', in *Heine Studien*, Düsseldorf, 1973

Wolff, A.V. Schmidt, 'Heine und Marx', in *Archiv für Kulturgeschichte*,
   Köln-Wien 54 (1972), pp. 143-52
Wülfing, Wulf, 'Schlagworte des Jungen Deutschland', in *Zeitschrift
   für deutsche Sprache* (1965-70), pp. 21-6

INDEX

Abrams, M.H. 32 n19
Adoratskij, V. 109, 117f
aesthetic education 52
Althusser, Louis 30, 31, 85, 89 n11,
    107, 115 n1, 118, 138, 149
Aristotle (*Rhetorics*) 118
Arnim, Bettina von 46
Athenäum (ed. Riedel 1841) 54,
    106 n7
Avineri, Shlomo 31 n14, 88 n1

Bachtin, Michail 57
Bauer, Bruno 24, 26, 57, 66 n22,
    70, 82, 93, 96, 98 ff, 107 ff,
    117 ff; and the censor 109;
    Allgemeine Literaturzeitung 83,
    107-16, 125 f; 'The Last Trump
    over Hegel 75, 83, 89 n4, 98 ff,
    108
Bauer, Edgar 18, 104
Béranger, P.J. 22
Berlin *Doktorklub* 57, 101
Bible 45, 47, 71, 84, 89 n4, 100,
    102 f, 107, 108, 111 ff, 114,
    116 n12, 117, 121 ff, 149;
    Hegel's *Phenomenology* as 'Bible'
    82, 125
Blum, Robert 129
Blumauer, Aloys 87
Bodi, Leslie 18 n2
Bonn *Poetenklub* 37, 120
Börne, Ludwig 94
Brecht, Bertolt 143-5
Brüggemann, Heinz 143-5
Buchbinder, Reinhold 84, 89 n7, 107
Buffon, Georges 28, 29

Callinicos, Alex 138
Campe, Julius 21, 23, 25
censorship:
    and style 17, 26 ff;
        and parody and satire *passim*;
        and silence *passim*; and wit
        26
    decrees: 1781 (June 11) 16;
        1818, Bavaria 20; 1819,
        Carlsbad 20, 21, 38 f, 42 n13,
        133; 1834 (April) 18; 1834

censorship—*cont.*
    (June) 21; 1835, Federal
    Decree against the Young
    Germany 21, 27 f, 34, 36, 37,
    39, 43, 44, 46, 48, 50, 61;
    1841 (8 December), ban on
    Campe 23, 25; 1841 (24
    December), 'Reform' 15, 23,
    26 ff, 95; 1843 (February) 17;
    1852, Heine's *Romanzero* 24;
    forms: as theft 28-9; Freudian 16;
    identity-giving 16 f; moral 20;
    private censure 16; self-
    censorship 21, 26 f, 30, 31,
    34, 48, 61; two forms of in
    editing Marx 11, 33, 54 ff,
    128, 149; 'Volkszensur' 16,
    18, 22
    periods: Enlightenment 11,
    15-19, 27, 50; Metternich 20,
    45-6; Napoleonic 20; Prussian
    11, 15, 20-32, 34; Roman
    (and census of property) 20,
    48; Young Germany 11, 15,
    22, 27 f, 31, 34, 36, 39, 43,
    50, 61
    structure: 'Index' 18;
    'Oberzensurgericht' 18;
    'Oberzensurkollegium' 17, 18,
    20, 21; Prussian ministries of
    17; 'Nachzensur' 21;
    'Vorzensur' 20, 21, 26, 82, 83,
    109, 110, 148;
Cervantes (*Don Quixote*) 57, 81 f,
    85, 121, 125, 143, 148, 152
Chamisso, Adalbert von 21 f, 35, 38,
    43, 48, 55, 64
'China' (Prussia) 40 f
Colletti, Lucio 101
Cornu, Auguste 11

Daniels, Dr Roland 55, 58, 61
Demetz, Peter 77 n1, 84, 91, 94
Deutsche Jahrbücher 23
Die Freien 26, 94, 100, 103 f
Die Stadtbote 91 ff, 96, 97 n2
Dingelstedt, Franz 25
Donaldson, Ian 49, 52 n4, 145 n9